BROKENNESS,
the Forgotten Factor
of Prayer

DEDICATION

This writing is dedicated to those who have made this journey with me over the years.

First and foremost, to Jesus Christ who has become more real to me in every way. I praise Him for His Wondrous, Glorious Presence in my life.

To my wife Margaret, my wonderful companion for over 40 years of laboring in the vineyard,

To my Board who pray and guide this ministry,

And especially for the many who intercede for this ministry daily,

From my heart --- THANK YOU!

BROKENNESS, the Forgotten Factor of Prayer

By
MICKEY BONNER
MICKEY BONNER EVANGELISTIC
ASSOCIATION
P.O. BOX 680368
HOUSTON, TEXAS 77268

ISBN 1-878578-12-X
© By Mickey Bonner
All Rights Reserved
Published by Mickey Bonner Evangelistic Association
P. O. Box 680368, Houston, Texas 77268
Printed in the United States of America

OTHER BOOKS BY MICKEY BONNER

- God Can Heal Your Mind
- Prayer is Warfare
- The Scriptural Way to Get Out of Debt
- Spiritual Warfare Manual
- What's Wrong with America?
- God's Answer to the Critical Christian
- Deliverance, the Children's Bread

SYLLABUSES

- Spiritual Warfare Seminar
- Spiritual Warfare Prayer Seminar
- Home and Family Seminar

BOOKLETS

- How to Find God's Will for My Life
- Awake America, the Russians are Here
- Job, A Lesson in Chastening
- Why I Like to Dance

For a free complete catalog of all of Brother Bonner's Books, Tapes, and Videos, write to: Mickey Bonner Evangelistic Association, P. O. Box 680368, Houston, Texas 77268.

ACKNOWLEDGMENTS

This book has been the greatest undertaking of my life and ministry. The warfare against the message has been, to say the least, incredible. It has been rewritten at least six times.

I want to thank all those who were in constant intercession for its completion.

Also, to my son Mickey II, who has designed - redesigned the cover, format, and layout.

Then, to Maggie Tribble and Karen Ogea who took what I felt was a completed manuscript and labored to make it grammatically correct.

To Diana Taylor, Linda Keklak, and Cynthia Parker who read and re-read the chapters and made suggestions that have been invaluable.

And then to Bonnie's Secretarial Service, thank you for your patience.

And foremost, I want to thank God, who has introduced me to every experience written. How wonderful the breaking.

INTRODUCTION

One of the major messages over the years in our Ministry has been the doctrine of brokenness. It is the foundation of all truth in the Scriptures. Without it, no man will truly see God.

When I began to write this manuscript, God graciously placed into my hands a wonderful book written by Edwin and Lillian Harvey, entitled Royal Insignia. It is a compilation of a lifetime of reading on their parts that produced excerpts from the writings and lives of many who had had the joyous experience of being broken before the Lord. I have used a number of these quotes throughout this writing to emphasize the truth of this imperative doctrine.

As I have prayed to be broken over the years, God has brought circumstances into my life that have created the crises that only He could resolve. As a result of these crises, I have found the Truth of His Sufficiency and His Grace, the Joy of His Presence, and the true beginning of Life in His Abundance. He is all we need. Oh, the Glory of the Cross, both His encounter on Calvary's Hill and our experience through Christ daily!

This writing is an effort to introduce to you the greatest experience you can have in a lifetime, and that is to "know Him and the Power of His Resurrection and the Fellowship of His Sufferings being made conformable to His Image."

The wonder of this experience is beyond words. How Great our God!

Mickey Bonner, 1994

TABLE OF CONTENTS

CHAPTER ONE

I WILL HEAR

I must begin with the fact that this writing will not be easy to accept. It is, however, an effort through prayer and conviction to introduce to you the only hope left in the world today. The dark clouds of history are gathering to conclude man's desire to rule himself. You, therefore, must face the final words given to you in the Bible, according to God's position on sin.

This is not a negative writing, but one that leads you to the glorious hope through a wondrous relationship with God. You will find this hope only through an extreme and concerted effort. The Scriptures say that you are to *present your body as living sacrifices, to labor to enter into the rest, to seek while He may be found, to knock and it shall be opened, and to assault the kingdom of God with violence.* This book, bathed in prayer, is an attempt to awaken you to the depth of true Christianity and to bring to your spiritual eyes the glories of tribulation, that in the end have their finished work in patience.

To the Child of God, these should be days of extreme seriousness; for the weight of what happens until Christ returns rests totally upon the shoulders of the Christian. Never before has the majority, through a belief in one God Jehovah, and His Son, Jesus Christ, so rapidly lost its position and place in a society. Because of the Laodicean age in which we live, we are increased with material goods and have need of nothing. We have lost contact with true holiness and the need for prayer and

God's intervention on a constant basis.

Due to the lack of serious praying, and consequently the loss of God's Power, there is now an acceleration of satanic dominion across the world system. Governments are taking a new look at the Christian doctrine and are beginning to state that we, as "cultists", are the causes of the present global problems, because we believe in the bodily return of Jesus Christ, and in being born-again.

Every form of media is attacking Christianity through motion pictures, music, television, and through every type of publication on a worldwide basis. Not since the first century, have we faced what we are seeing now. It will get worse! These media channels promote the idea that Christianity, now reported to be the root of all evil, is responsible for the cold war, poverty, crime, discrimination, child abuse, homophobia, and many other radical concepts that destroy the process of international unity. The world, in response, says that we are destroying it. These are truly *the beginning of sorrows,*" (*Matthew 24:8*).

Now, in many parts of the world, as the religious system endeavors to build more and better churches, it becomes against the law to be a believer in Jesus Christ and walk in Biblical attributes. In America, lawyers are being trained in how to sue churches. Freedoms, on a daily basis, are being eradicated and removed as those who feel that a one-world system, and a one-world government involving a one-world religion, is the only hope for existence in the twenty-first century. There is also a major move against the establishment of the home as a family unit, dictating that the home must be destroyed in order that the state may become the moral, religious, and parental guide for bringing up all children. Thus is the thinking and concept of those in the one-world system: to bring all persons under one rule by starting with children at an early age, guiding their minds and eradicating true Biblical Christianity.

RELIGION HAS NO PLACE IN RIGHTEOUSNESS

Religion has no place in righteousness. Its works are as the birth of a stillborn whose life ceased in the womb. In fact, there is but one hope to hold back the swelling, overwhelming tide of Satan's move to destroy all elements of truth in righteousness and to totally remove the Blood of Jesus Christ from all religious doctrine. But God has never failed us. He is immutable. His Word has remained true from the moment that it was breathed into the life of man, that it might be written upon pages and presented as inspired. All of God's revelations, as well as proclamations, have come to pass in His own time. Now we face what He declares will happen in these final moments of history. You and I are alive at their happening!

I have studied the end-time message for nearly forty years and my heart continues to be especially quickened lately by one line and phrase: *"Even so, come, Lord Jesus,"* (*Revelation 22:20*). I have preached with violence the message of the Second Coming. I have witnessed the fact that there is an evidence of God built into every human being, (*Romans 1:19*), and that there could come a revealing to their hearts by the Power of the Word, His Spirit, and Person. Then, the Holy Spirit would say to their spirit, "This is true," and they, breaking under conviction, would cry out in repentance before God, seeking to be born again—only then to be filled with the Glory and Wonder of True Salvation. How Great is our God!

While all other doctrines and philosophies have failed over the centuries, God's Word has remained steadfast. It is an element so strong that nothing shall penetrate, cut, or chip it away. It becomes even mightier when attacked. Satan, through writings of non-Christians, has made an extreme move to destroy the Bible in every way. And yet in all of the onslaughts, it has become more powerful by the test of time. It is the foundation of all that is and all that ever shall be. All of its claims have come to pass or are coming to pass.

HEAL THEIR LAND

It is from the position of God's promises that I am so impressed to write this book, with an effort to characterize within it the promise of what can happen at this point in history based on what we will face in coming days. We have been given the option of the greatest victory that could ever be known. We can experience pure joy in the midst of what is coming. It is exciting to be here at Christ's return! In this first chapter, we will show what God commands of us in order for His Glory to fall; for it is Biblically promised in this period of history, but only by God's conditions.

It is my personal feeling, through study, that in the midst of all that is transpiring, there can be a wedge driven into history; not to stop the events of a dying world, but to bring the Holy Spirit in such staggering power that revival would reach across the world's system, sweeping millions into the Kingdom of God. In fact, we are promised that *"where sin did abound, grace did much more abound."* God pledges this and gives to us Scriptural positions in numerous places in the Word. Especially in **II Chronicles 7:14** do we find that, regardless of the issues faced by believers, God states:

"... If my people, which are called by my name,

shall humble themselves and pray and seek my face and turn from their wicked ways, then will I hear from heaven and will forgive their sin and will heal their land."

That promise alone gives us hope that if we meet the requirements of God, regardless of the circumstance, He will intervene with His Spirit. It is in the light of this that we begin by stating His Promises to all who will meet His prerequisite. The world system faces utter devastation and annihilation. Not only are there nuclear fears, but there is no way in the present population explosion that people can be fed. Now AIDS, forming within the bodies of people as in an incubator, is being spread, almost unchecked, to new and fertile beings. Research now states that the virus is mingling with other diseases and is further developing into a hybrid state that is even more deadly and uncontrollable. It is also known that AIDS is no longer being propagated by sexual encounter alone. Based on research, we are told that for a period of time, it can live in a dormant state in the form of mucous, tear drops, and blood. In other words, it can live outside of the body for a number of days, waiting for a chance encounter with an innocent person passing by. This, I believe, is the end time pestilence spoken of by the Scriptures.

History is getting darker as we come to the end of the age. You say, "Is there any hope?" Yes, there is wonderful hope! But it is only through God, and His ways are not our ways. His Spirit will intervene into the hearts of men according to Biblical principles only, because God never changes. As I will state many times in this writing, God's Word is immutable, meaning that it "never changes."

WHAT MAKES GOD WORK?

We have shared the wonderful verse of *II Chronicles 7:14*. How many times, however, do we have a tendency to take a passage out of text and develop around it a reasoned form of righteousness that eventually equates into a religious stand? By that, I mean we try to get God to join us, rather than our joining Him.

Let's begin in the Scriptures and see if there is still hope for revival. Without prayer one is without God. He moves only through His Will, in and by prayer. To understand how God gets into a matter, let's begin in *II Chronicles 7:9*. Here we find that "... *they made a solemn assembly.*" I will address this subject a number of times in this book as a foundation for God's intervention in the tragedies of the day. The definition of a "solemn assembly" is a "serious time of getting together, praying, and waiting upon the Lord." A solemn assembly is a crucial gathering of those with one heart in brokenness before God, that in their desperation they might be able to hear from Him. This is the reality of Upper Room praying as in Acts 1. They stayed and prayed until God answered as the Holy Spirit came. It has to happen at this time in history.

Again, a solemn assembly is when Christians get together in desperate prayer, yielding and believing for God's intervention, knowing that He has to come. The conditions for this type of prayer are then given in the *14th* verse of *II Chronicles 7*. First of all, the Bible states, *"If my people which are called by my name..."* It must be noted that after the Holy Spirit came on the day of Pentecost, the Apostles and all believers were filled with the Presence and Power of God. The Holy Spirit is in us as well for one reason, and that is to build within, (from the inside out), the Ministry of Christ and

His Will. For that to happen, we must be humbled and broken before God. In that bent, contrite state, when we pray, our prayer will then declare, "I must have you, God. I must have you." From that position, and that position only, with overwhelming desire will we turn from our wicked ways.

Jonathan Edwards wrote, "Nothing sets a person so much out of the devil's reach as humility." It is only from that place that God promises, *"I will hear from heaven and will forgive their sins and will heal their land."* Beloved friend, do you realize that the Christian holds the key to the Spirit of God returning to the hearts of the people in this world system? Again, I will attempt to show that, historically, in every move of God that has carried the name of real revival, there has always been one person who prayed—one broken, burdened individual before God, who, through his life, believed the truth that II Chronicles would come alive.

In spite of what many are saying today, we can still have revival. There can be a hindrance of the evil that is consuming us even as God continues the preparation of the coming of the Lord Jesus by aligning the nations into their places in final conflict. There can be millions upon millions of precious souls born into the Kingdom of God, if but a few will make the transition from religious principles to brokenness. Remember, religion is an effort to try to force God to work according to one's own will and not His. It will take the tears of shattered hearts rather than the fetish prayer clubs that are forming worldwide. We must be broken. We must!

Again, so much is being written today about how to get God involved in religious activities. Yet none of these activities work because they deal with pride through works rather than the Person of Jesus Christ. Dr. MacLaren wrote, "Self confidence shuts a man out from the help of God, and so shuts him out from the source of power." Real prayer is simply the Power of God through the broken hearts of His People. We will have more to say regarding brokenness later in this writing.

There is a book in the Old Testament that deals directly with this exact time of history in which we live today. It is the Book of Joel. In this inspired revelation, we are given the exact circumstances and happenings of this present time, and how through our obedience, these events could be altered. God gives the way of eternal life even in the midst of looming darkness. All it takes is one true intercessor. The Holy Spirit can, through the life of one broken individual, flood light into the blindness of human hearts. We need one believer who will not tolerate religion, but will live in righteousness; one abandoned to the Lord—just one.

Charles Spurgeon stated: "When a man is sincerely humble and never ventures to touch so much as a grain of praise, there is scarcely any limit to what God will do for him. Humility makes us ready to be blessed by the God of all grace, and fits us to deal efficiently with our fellow men."

THE WONDER OF IT ALL

To begin the process of God's visitation to us, we find in *Joel 1:14* the only procedure for the issuance of victory. He says: *"Sanctify ye a fast. Call a solemn assembly."* Now, in other writings, I have dealt with the doctrine of fasting. In our book, Prayer is Warfare, we have explained that it is God's process to bring the believer into being set free from bondage. Fasting is still imperative today. The profound truth of this doctrine is that it is not to change the Will of God or to force Him to do something. But it is for the individual fasting to be brought into brokenness. In the process, flesh is broken and consumed by the Holy Spirit, that it might be presented back to God as a living sacrifice, ready for His Will to be done. Fasting is the lost art in the church as we are so increased with goods and have need of nothing. Who wants to deny the body anything?

In the wonderful book of Isaiah, God lays out His position on fasting. He states that it is not to be instigated by convenience, but through brokenness over one's own sin. It is promised that through the process God will bring change to the life of the individual. We are not to fast for strife and debate as God says in *Isaiah 58:4-5*, or to make our voice heard on high. Fasting is not God's doorbell. It is not given to us to get His attention. It is, however, an inward desire to bring our bodies into subjection, that we might present them as living sacrifices back to the Lord. Neither is fasting initiated to gain the attention of man. In fact, it was the religious custom in that day to make your fast obvious by either marking your face with soot from the cooking area or walking around with a fallen countenance so that others might say, "He is fasting. Look how righteous he is."

These are serious and desperate days in history. We must come to God in the acceptable way of the Lord. It is our only hope. Our present system has failed. God's judgment is beginning to rain upon us. He further instructs us in *Isaiah 58:6*, that He has chosen the fast "to loose the bands of wickedness," to "control the wicked one." He reminds us that fasting will replace the heavy burdens with praise, as we bring into our tribulation the Presence of God, allowing His Grace to become joyfully sufficient. It is only by God's Power that the oppressed are released of their oppression and freed. Satan was defeated at Calvary by the Blood of Jesus Christ. If those with consuming sins would yield their bodies to God for His intervention and cleansing through fasting, Isaiah says the "yoke" would be broken. Again, Satan is defeated. My beloved, revival would come globally if some would answer the call to brokenness. By doing what God says, we could have worldwide revival before Christ comes. It has to happen. Billions are lost without Christ. Yes, that's right, billions.

Fasting brings through you the ministry of the Spirit of God to others. As your spiritual vision clears, you begin to see what God sees through the eyes of the Holy Spirit, (*Ephesians 1:18*). From there you begin to live by the Holy Spirit regarding others; for Biblical fasting brings the light of God exploding in your heart. Isaiah says, *"It comes like the morning."* While in that transformed position, your own flesh or personal life is no longer the consuming desire of your being. From that broken, contrite state of denial of the body's fleshly desires you will begin craving the Will of God, having been able in the self-denied state, to hear from God in your spirit man. Your prayer, under those conditions, becomes the Will of God as you, in essence, say, *"Thy kingdom come, thy will be done, on earth as it is in heaven."*

The secret of prayer is being able to hear and agree with the Father in His Will, as Jesus did in John, chapter 5. For the key to all praying is receiving in your spirit as Jesus said in *John 5:30*. He states, *"I can of mine own self do nothing; as I hear I judge..."* When you are broken through true fasting, you will begin to sense the presence of God's Spirit in your life and the wondrous place of worship in the Spirit, and by the Spirit, (*Philippians 3:3, Amplified*). You will be able to understand His Voice. Also, you will find your negative confession and your desire to listen to gossip abhorrent, as we will address in later chapters. You, through the eyes of Jesus, will suddenly see men as He sees them, saved or lost, and you'll weep. You will experience as the song says, "The wonder of it all."

God promises, as a result of fasting, His Life in you, and His Ministry through you, in agreement with His Will and purpose for your birth upon this earth, (*Ephesians 2:10*). He further promises to be your guide, and in the midst of all tribulation He pledges to make a way of escape. In His daily presence, you will be like "a spring of water whose waters fail not", as springing up within you is the fountain of life that has its source in eternity, (*John 4:14*). Then, through your life, God shall bring restoration and will raise up the foundations of many generations. His Ministry through you will be, *"the repairer of the breach, the restorer of paths to dwell in."*

Those are the promises to you in *Isaiah 58*, if you will involve yourself in the fast that God has chosen. Fasting will break the body's (flesh) control over the soul, resulting in a union between your human spirit and the Holy Spirit. As I said to you before, fasting, along with brokenness in prayer is the lost position in the church. People today are more interested in the time than they are the times. They are more burdened about 12:01 Sunday afternoon and getting out of the service as quickly as possible than they are with what is happening. And when you try to tell them, they become *"dull of hearing,"* (*Hebrews 5:11*). No one wants any bad news, but in this case it would be good news.

My beloved, these are the most desperate times in history, and yet it is a time when God would move in a mighty way if His conditions were met. With this promise in mind, let's look again at *Joel 1:14*. God says:

"Sanctify ye a fast. Call a solemn assembly. Gather the elders and all the inhabitants of the land into the house of the Lord your God and cry unto the Lord."

Through the verses of Joel we begin to have insight of what God would do at this place in time if we would meet His condition.

In *chapter 2, the first verse*, He continues by stating:

"Blow ye the trumpet in Zion, and sound an alarm in my holy mountain: let all the inhabitants in the land tremble: for the day of the Lord cometh, for it is nigh at hand."

Again, understand that this prophetic book is for today. As men's hearts continue to fail, you will see that those whose seeds were planted upon hard, dry ground will fall away. Their decisions for Christ originated from the soul and not from the spirit, (*Matthew 13:4-8*). And yet, these same seeds (the Word of God) planted in fallow (broken) ground continue to bear the fruit of righteousness. It is to those who are truly born again that I write this book on brokenness. This is a "hard saying," but this truth must be understood in order to fulfill God's Will in these final days.

As we progress, we read that God lays out for us the conditions that must be met for Him to move against the tidal wave of Satan's end time world system. He can pour out His Spirit upon all flesh. His moving will come in only one way. It will not be by great singing, concerts, or music. It will not come by dynamic preaching. It will only happen when men become so broken before God that their only hope is Jesus Christ and His intervention. God moves only through tears of brokenness. Historically, as well as Biblically, we find that man's view of God's Will is seen only through tears. His ways are not our ways.

He tells us this in the following words. *Joel 2:12-19* states:

"Therefore also now, saith the Lord, turn ye even to me with all your heart, and with fasting, and with weeping, and with mourning: And rend your heart, and not your garments, and turn unto the Lord your God: for he is gracious and merciful, slow to anger, and of great kindness, and repenteth him of the evil. Who knoweth if he will return and repent, and leave a blessing behind him; even a meat offering and a drink offering unto the lord your God? Blow the trumpet in Zion, sanctify a fast, call a solemn assembly: Gather the people, sanctify the congregation, assemble the elders, gather the children, and those that suck the breasts: let the bridegroom go forth of his chamber, and the bride out of her closet. Let the priests, the ministers of the Lord, weep between the porch and the altar, and let them say, Spare thy people, O Lord, and give not thine heritage to reproach, that the heathen should rule over them: Therefore should they say among the people, Where is their God? Then will the Lord be jealous for his land, and pity his people. Yea, the Lord will answer and say unto his people, Behold, I will send you corn, and wine, and oil, and ye shall be satisfied therewith: and I will no more make you a reproach among the heathen."

Herein is the All Eternal God with heaven's directions for the restoration of His Will to this world. Remember, this book is about brokenness and the wondrous walk with God that is found in a realm beyond all fleshly understanding. Therefore, in these verses, we find His declaration of what must happen for Him to act upon and change any given situation sovereignly. Beloved, I do urge you to remember that He is still God and everything is at His feet. Everything.

In looking at God's plan for His Will to be done, here is what He states in these verses. *"Therefore also now saith the Lord, turn ye even to me with all of your heart."* Again, to parallel this, God said in **II Chronicles 7:14**, **"If my people which are called by name shall humble themselves."** In later chapters, we will deal with the word "contriteness," which God commands must be in the life of the believer if He is to work in and through his life. Only from that place of brokenness will He resurrect within the individual the Life of His Son and His Ministry. We are commanded, in order for God to move through us upon this world system today, to come back to God as a living sacrifice, holy, acceptable (at the level of His Holiness, not our religion), and we are to bring our bodies into total subjection to the Spirit and Will of God. In doing so, we make them one. Our flesh is not to be king. God takes that place over us. It is a commanded effort on our part to force or labor ourselves into His Will. In actuality, it is the difference between the Bible being the milk of the word, or meat, depending on our level of brokenness, (*Hebrews 5:12-14*). Babies cannot ingest anything but liquid. The same is true of the church today. Men cannot endure sound doctrine. They hate the Truth of God and will fight against it.

THE VIEW FROM THE TOP

For many years, we have been teaching spiritual warfare

in the fundamentalist church. As a result, many critics within the learned realms of academics have accused us of teaching foolishness. Yet, the explosion of witchcraft, the youthful suicides, (especially in the families of Pastors and other Christians), brought on by rock music, coupled with the new age, has suddenly found the "wise ones" devoid of abilities to doctrinally help in these areas, and the Church is being overcome and destroyed. It has lost its power to stand against what is happening. It is non-praying. Unbroken leadership is leading the blind.

To walk with God, we must move toward Him by the force of prayer until we are overwhelmed with His Glory in our souls. God will not perform His Work through us unless we are broken before the Lord. Therefore, it is our place to go after Him. We must force ourselves to open the Word of God and read it until the Spirit of God begins to quicken us in the inner man with His Power. Then, as we begin to feast and grow on His Truths, we find we cannot put it down. Such are the results and experiences when we fight and capture our own flesh, presenting it back to God, (*Romans 12:1-2*).

In *Romans 8:7*, the Bible says: *"The carnal mind is enmity against God,"* and that word "enmity" means "hostile". Satan will involve you in religious activity to keep you busy, in order to stop you from prayer and from the truth-revealing study and Power of the Word of God.

In the light of this, not only are you to bring your life in sacrifice to God, but you are also to fast, a true test of obedience, (*Joel 2:12*). Many say that fasting is an Old Testament principle. This profound doctrine is alive in the New Testament as well. Again, it is given as a breaking of the soul that you may be able to present your body back to God, a living sacrifice.

Joel 2 continues to say that we are to come *"with weeping."* God's sequence of visitation upon His people first occurs when we bring the body back into God's control. Then we will be broken through tears. The evident sign of Christ's control in your life is when you see what God sees in you and in your spirit. You then feel what God feels, because you now see your true self as God sees you. A devastation of your pride will result. You will be broken over your own life. It has to happen within us for God to come back on the scene. We must be broken or all is lost.

He goes on to say, "... *and rend your heart and not your garments.*" Now, that really sounds Old Testament. But please understand, back in that day and time if the religious leaders saw something that they felt was a personal affront to their religious beliefs, as a show of aversion to it they would rip the garments from their bodies to reveal their violent disdain. So it was with the ministry of Christ on the earth. In defiance to the religious authority, He was hated then as He is today. And beloved, when you submit to God your complete life, get ready to be misunderstood and hated for His Name's sake.

May I say to you also that, when you move into brokenness, one of the evidences that God is conforming you to His Image is that many will think you have lost your mind or "gone off of the deep end." I'm talking about those within the religious circle with which you are involved.

Recently, a very godly brother in the Lord, was conducting a revival. He, in his deep love for God, is a broken man and ministers with anointing. He was speaking on the subject of brokenness. A pastor was visiting the service. Later, the visiting pastor commented to the pastor of the church, "With all the troubles of today, his message should be upbeat." My beloved, we have preached such an uplifting, compromising, meet-you-where-you-are message that it has lost its power. Consequently, Satan has consumed the church, and its prayer remains powerless. Everybody wants to play and nobody wants to pray. They will, however, want to pray as the world's system soon decays and freedoms are lost.

Believer, if you're going to become free in your spirit, you must take an aggressive position of praise, in the midst of all tribulation. This will increase your faith as God moves in and you are overcome by His Spirit, seeing His Hand working in the matter. From that position, you will want to study the Word. You will fall in love with Jesus Christ in such an overwhelming way, that when confronted with sin, you will have a complete desire to turn away. The Holy Spirit will say within you, "Don't," and in your oneness with Him, you will fight against your flesh in order to retain the wonderful relationship you have with Christ.

Religion that takes its roots from the Bible, but denies its authority, will be the instrument that will condemn the Christian someday as the one-world system continues to be pieced together. Its leaders will rend their garments at our "born again" faith and say we are the causes of all the problems in the world. It is coming. But, in the midst of all that will transpire, we can still see millions saved, and hinder its destructive onslaught, if we follow God's Plan and Will.

For this to be accomplished by God, you, believer, must rend your heart. You must be broken before the Lord. For God has placed the Scriptures of Joel in a perfect sequence in that you must stand before God weeping and broken over the circumstances at hand. When you get serious with God and your heart is devastated, the verse says that you will "turn unto the Lord, your God." You will, for He is the only hope. Why? Because, in that posture of contriteness, your eyes will be opened, and for the first time your inner man will see the true perspective of all the events that are occurring. You will find yourself, as Paul stated, *"seated in the heavenlies"* and, beloved, <u>the view is always better from the top.</u>

Cults exist today that demonically consume the minds of their followers by having them repeat phrases over and over until they become self-hypnotic. A religious spirit then enters. Many times, it will be one called Jesus, for there are spirit demons by that name operating in the world system. We find this in *II Corinthians 11:3-4*. The results are found in that same chapter, verses 12 through 15. It all adds up to what is Biblically stated as the scene at the Great White Throne, as many will cry out, *"Have we not cast out demons in thy name? Have we not done many wonderful works in thy name?"* only to hear the response from the Father, *"Depart from me ye cursed. I never knew you,"* (*Matthew 7:22-23*).

Beloved, remember that all Christianity is the activity of Jesus Christ through your life, (*John 5:30*). Don't look at your religious experience and think that you have arrived at righteousness, because it might have the working of a gift. Satan is the counterfeiter. Always remember, the only evident sign of spiritual maturity is answered prayer: hearing from God and then understanding and agreeing. If you have no answered prayer, I would seek God to find out the exact position of my life in the Lord. First, am I saved? Second, am I maturing to the place of hearing and understanding the language of God through His Word and by His Spirit? (*John 5:30*).

Continuing in Joel, we find that God is gracious, merciful, and slow to anger. He is of great kindness. We are told that if His conditions are met, He will intervene and change the direction of an individual or even, as seen in the Old Testament, a total national system, *"and repenteth him of the evil."* God promises to meet us if we place Him first in our lives. If we do, we can and will see a great move of God in this end time. He again tells us, in verse 15, to "blow the trumpet in Zion, to sanctify a fast, to call a solemn assembly". Herein is our only hope. We must, as individuals, be broken before the Lord. We are to call the people together who are desperately serious and committed to God. He commands us to come together, to pray and to assemble the elders. It is the imperative. To do what? Again, to pray. To fast. To weep before God, that He pour His Spirit out upon this land. Nothing else is going to work. We must get serious. Without it, there is no hope, (Psalm 9:17).

WHERE IS THEIR GOD?

In *Joel 2:16-17*, He gives us the clearest picture of what is tragically wrong today. He states that until *"the priests, the ministers of the Lord, weep between the porch and the altar,"* and literally in brokenness cry out, *"Spare thy people, O Lord, and give not thine heritage to reproach that the heathen should rule over them,"* we will never see revival.

At this writing, I've been in close to 3,000 Meetings. I share with people that I am so old that I can remember when Christians came to the altar of a church and wept openly. I can recall one night in a service some thirty-five years ago, at the beginning of our evangelistic ministry, a husband and wife coming and kneeling. They were sobbing in such brokenness that I finally went to the pastor and asked him if he wanted me to minister to them. He said, "Oh, no, Brother Bonner. Just leave them alone. They have a nine year old boy who is lost and they're praying for his salvation." Have we forgotten what happens to a person when he dies without Christ? Hell is still as real as your heartbeat.

I recall another service, one night in a church in a country setting. We gave an invitation, and a farmer came forward dressed in overalls, and he was crying. He fell on his knees and was broken and weeping so loudly that it was almost a hindrance to the altar-call. People, upon hearing, would look up at him and then bow their heads again in prayer. Finally, wondering why the pastor had not gone over to pray with him, I whispered, "What should we do about this man?" He said, "Oh, Brother Bonner, he's all right. He teaches junior boys and he has several that are lost without Christ in his class and he's burdened for their condition. He is interceding."

Folks, I have not seen that in years. Where are the tears? They're gone. Our precious pastors are being trained in how to build, as one writer says, "user friendly churches," but not how to build the Kingdom. These men come out of college or seminary completely saturated with academics and truths that are taught to the mind and not married to the spirit. They move into the world system of denominational religious politics where men control and must keep their organization self-perpetuated. Now there is nothing wrong with denominations or groups of people who have banded together to increase missions. But when it reaches the state of politics for perpetuation, it loses its original concept and the power of its origin, which is the coming together of people for the purposes of having a single doctrinal truth and developing a greater outreach to bring people to Christ. Denominations, for the most part, are birthed upon good ideals, but over a period of time, begin to compromise their convictions until, by corruption, they have totally lost their original vision and power. As the Bible says, *"they measuring themselves by themselves and comparing themselves among themselves, are not wise" (II Corinthians 10:12)*. They begin to grow inward. Until our pastors are broken and begin weeping before God, revival cannot and will not come.

Leonard Ravenhill states in <u>Why Revival Tarries</u>, "POOR GOD! He does not get much out of it all! Then why doesn't God fulfill His blessed and yet awful promise and spew us out of mouth? We have failed. We are filthy. We love men's praise. We seek our own. Oh God, lift us out of this rut and this rot! Bless us with breakings! Judgment must begin with us preachers!"

Occasionally, some of these preachers called of God will go off to a spiritual conference or perhaps journey through some great cataclysmic experience in their lives. In this climate, they yield everything back to God. Because of this complete abandonment to the Lord, they come to the end of themselves. They discover a new level, a new place, a new glory in Christ. It is called the filling of the Holy Spirit, (*Ephesians 5:18*), or the sufficiency and consuming of their lives by His Grace in the time of their need.

They come back to their churches broken. They stand in their pulpits anointed. Suddenly, from that filled posture, many members become gripped by the Power of the Word of God and become convicted of their sin by the Holy Spirit. It is in this climate that other (religious) church members become ignited in anger, (*Matthew 13:24-30*). Those angered members begin to sow seeds of strife through a fury of words, because their own sinful lives have been revealed. They even say of the minister, "Something has happened to him. He's no longer Baptist (or Methodist, etc.) What's happened to our preacher? He doesn't act right. I feel so uneasy when he preaches." So, Satan begins the work of witchcraft, (*II Chronicles 33:6*), which is the Hebrew word Kashaph that means "whispering," and the pastor either turns back toward the flesh to save his ministry and salary, or he becomes an even more broken man as he is rejected or finally ousted many times by his own members. It is either revival or revolution. God, however, one way or another, can always be found in the midst of our failure, for from that place He becomes our sufficiency by His glory. He now can begin His Ministry through us.

If you are a Pastor reading this, and you have experienced what I have just described, (as I have many times), I beg you to "turn your lemons into lemonade." Yield to God your life and ministry. Surrender your complete being to Him. He loves you and has a work that is His Will in and through you. Make full restoration of your ministry back to Him and abandon yourself totally to Christ. Begin to fast, study, and most of all pray to be broken. From that place you will begin a true ministry—His. In fact, from this position, revival will become revolution.

W. L. Watkinson writes:

"The sense of failure is acutest where the aim is the highest, and the catalog of defeat suggests the grandeur of enterprise. Think of the enemies we challenge, our vast ambition, our immense field of action, the difficult elements in which we work, and no wonder that we know most of the sense of failures, and feel failure most keenly.

But our failures are infinite successes, our defeats victories, our martyrs conquerors; we faint only to prevail, we die to live in resurrection, power and beauty. He who is the same yesterday, today, and forever knows all this. It is His own program; and He is not disheartened."

The same message, said in another way, is in this poem by Fredric Lucian Hosner:

By failure and defeat made wise,
We come to know at length,
What strength within our weakness lies,
What weakness in our strength.

What inward peace is born of strife,
What power of being spent;
What wings unto our upward life,
Is noble discontent.

O Lord, we need thy shaming look,
That burns all low desire;
The discipline of Thy rebuke,
Shall be refining fire!

In the light of this, we're going to show you in this writing, Biblically, that God has never performed a continuing ministry through any individual who has not been broken. I appeal to you to get excited about who you are in Christ. I urge you to take God at His Word as expressed in Joel. In fact, I beg you to begin to fast and pray to be broken, that God, through the cracks of your life, can minister the light of His Will into the hearts and needs of your people. Seek Him to renew a right spirit within you, (*Psalms 51:10*). Again, He says, "*Until the priests, the ministers of the Lord, weep between the porch and the altar*," the world will say, "*Where is their God?*'" Beloved, He still uses the "*foolishness of preaching,*" (*I Corinthians 1:21*). It is only through brokenness, however, that He brings the anointing. In your surrender to His calling you took on the responsibility of His Will and will be held accountable, (*James 3:1-2, I Peter 5:1-5*).

I would then urge you, as an individual church member reading this book, to begin to pray, not only for your brokenness, but to entreat also that your pastor be broken before the Lord.

Do not let fear or Satan's accusations keep you from this. Did you have an earthly father that you loved and trusted? If you could trust your earthly father and his love for you, can you not trust your Heavenly Father? Once more, do not let Satan accuse you, causing you to say, "If I submit to God and ask to be broken, He will take from me my health or loved ones." That is a lie and an accusation from the enemy. God always deals in the area of your greatest need. If it is pride, get ready to be embarrassed, until you can not only praise God for the circumstances in which He has placed you, but also until He becomes sufficient in the matter, through praise. Then, not only will you have learned a truth, but you will have grown in that area. From growth, you will be birthed into a higher step of maturity or faith. The transition will be worth the lesson learned.

We must begin to pray for preachers to be broken before God and weep for a return of His Spirit in their lives and churches. You see, pastors are men called of God. They are called by Him to preach the Gospel as the imperative of their life. If they can do anything else, then they need to do it, (*James 1:18*). If preaching is the only hope and direction for their lives and they are compelled to submit, then it is a true calling. It is a gift from God. Also, they will be held accountable in judgment for what they say and do before God, (*II Corinthians 5:10*). The Bible says: *"My brethren, be not many masters, knowing that we shall receive the greater condemnation"* (*James 3:1*). In praying for them to be broken, you will actually be doing them the greatest favor that could ever be done to them. It purifies their message from hearsay or education to direct ministry by the Holy Spirit. To stand before God in judgment, not having done His Will, will be tragic for them. As was the coin or buried talent spoken of in Scripture, so will they bury their true ministry in fear. For the standard of the church today, by the world's judgment, is not how much of the Power of God is upon it, but how much money and how many people are in it. As one friend of mine said many years ago, "Today you judge a church by its nickels and noses."

Pity the preacher who pastors without power, but preaches with purpose and plan to promote his personal presence before people for his own pleasure to build his place in ministry. (You forgive that play on words. I enjoy doing that in preaching.) I personally experienced preaching without power, first as a pastor and then as an evangelist. I preached to please the listener's ear and to build my ministry. For anything to be done in Truth, it is imperative that the ministers weep in brokenness and cry out to God to spare the people. Again, God will hold the pastors of today in greater condemnation because they are not broken and anointed by prayer! The results of their powerless place is found then in *Joel 2:17*, as it states that the world will say: *"Wherefore should they say among the people, Where is their God?"* Where is the God of Abraham? Where is the God of Isaac? Where is the God of miracles and power today? God wants, at this present time, to do a work so miraculous and profound that it will startle men into faith and belief. It can happen. But it will not happen until we, as believers, are broken before God, especially Pastors.

Beloved, let not the world say of us, "Where is their God?" May His Glory in these final moments of history be so poured out that the people of our Nation would be saved through the prayer of the believers, as did happen in the revival in the Hebrides. Through the intercession of two people, Satan lost an entire population, for revival swept that area over a period of two years. It is recorded history. It was truly a visitation from God.

Now, what are the results when the people become broken and pastors weep? The Bible says in *Joel 2:18*: *"Then*

will the Lord be jealous for His land and pity His people."
Oh, my beloved, it must happen. It has got to happen. We must
pray to be broken, and if we're humbled before God He will heal
our land. He said He would.

In fact, when you parallel *II Chronicles 7:14* with
Joel 2:18, the promise is the same. Again, He says:

> *"If my people which are called by my name
> shall humble themselves and pray and seek my
> face, and turn from their wicked ways, then
> will I hear from heaven, and forgive their sin,
> and will heal their land."*

Now, in comparing *II Chronicles 7:14* with *verse 18* in
Joel 2, a common statement is noted: *"Then will the Lord be
jealous for His land."* Do you see that all is not lost? Joel is a
prophecy written for today. It is the period in which we live
presently ... right NOW. God declares that something can be
done. I am not a fatalist. I am not hidden away on some
mountain waiting with my precious family for the Lord to
return. I am fighting for revival. It has to happen. Billions are
without Christ. Something has to be done and only a visitation
of God's Spirit will do it. Oh, my beloved, pray to be broken. It
could be "Amen" to us if we return to God in brokenness. He
says: *"my groaning is not hid from thee,"* (*Psalm 38:9*).
Exodus 2:24 states, *"God heard their groaning and God
remembered."* C. H. Spurgeon said, "Groanings which cannot
be uttered are often prayers which cannot be refused." James
Caughey in his short poem expressed:

> "My powerful groans thou canst not bear.
> Nor stand the violence of Prayers.
> My Prayer omnipotent."

Read this wonderful poem as many times as it takes to consume your spirit. Then, you must understand that prayer, (or judgment,) is God's entrance into a circumstance. His entrance, however, does not come through rote prayers, or the repetition of prayers, but through brokenness: praying the Will of God as spoken to the heart of men by God's Spirit. He will have pity upon His people, the Bible says. We, as Christians, are His. We are called by His Name. We that are born again are the ones—and the only ones—that can have answered prayer. It must, however, be accomplished "with groanings which cannot be uttered." It must be by intercession, (*Exodus 2:23-25; 3:9*). There has to be a visitation of God's Spirit poured out on us now. It has to happen .

POUR OUT MY SPIRIT

If we meet God's standards, we will see His glorious, wonderful promise! Beloved, I know I shall see it in my lifetime, for I truly believe Him when He says in *Joel 2:28, 29*:

> *"And it shall come to pass afterward, that I will pour out my spirit upon all flesh; and your sons and your daughters shall prophesy, your old men shall dream dreams and your young men shall see visions: And also upon the servants and upon the handmaids in those days will I pour out my spirit."*

It is the burden of my heart that revival come. I've never, in all of my ministry, conducted so many meetings as I am now. In my spirit, I know that someday I shall go to a place and not be able to leave. Somewhere, revival is going to break out. It could be in the United States or in the Philippines where we also have an established ministry. Europe or Africa could be the location. Wherever it is, I'm excitedly anticipating this encounter with God. It is the desire of my heart to see this move of the Spirit as it is promised by Him.

Oh, God, pour out Your Spirit. Break our hearts. We must be broken before the Lord. Please break us!

Here is a poem that has a profound message relevant to this book's intent. The author is unknown.

> "One by one He took them from me,
> All the things I valued most.
> Until I was empty-handed,
> Every glittering toy was lost.
> And I walked earth's highways grieving.
> In my ranks of poverty,
> Until I heard His voice inviting,
> 'Lift those empty hands to me.'
> Then I turned my hands toward heaven,
> And He filled them with a store,
> Of all His own transcended riches,
> Until they could contain no more.
> At last I comprehended,
> With my stupid mind and dull,
> That God cannot pour out His riches,
> Into hands already full."

Such is the message as we go on with this writing. Now, in order that you may receive these truths, pray to be broken now. Come empty handed. It is wonderful. In fact, it will be the genesis of your life.

CHAPTER TWO

THE BEGINNING OF ALL TRUE MINISTRY

The Scriptures demonstrate many examples of God's movement upon the lives of individuals to create within them the desperate need for God's Presence and the consciousness of His Will. Brokenness, for the most part, is the means by which God conveys maturity and develops character. Discipline in the lives of the believers brings each into an abandonment of self to God in prayer. Then, through breaking, they discover God's Righteousness as they are driven toward Him in desperate need. The capacity to know God, which is built into every human being, (**Romans 1:19**), is subsequently filled with joy unspeakable and obedience to His Will.

With this in mind, look at the story of Job. Job is perhaps one of the greatest (books) on brokenness in the Bible, and is a classic example of the story of a man who experienced true breaking. As you study his life, you see the sovereign hand of God reconstructing a man's soul through contriteness, to develop within him a true ministry. The purpose of Job's breaking was to conform him to the image of God, (**Colossians 3:10**). Let's look at the Scriptural account of his transition and see.

The Bible begins, in *Job 1:1*:

"There was a man in the land of Uz, whose name was Job; and that man was perfect and upright and one that feared God and eschewed evil."

Already we have an insight of the depth and quality of his being. As we begin to look at this account, we will discover that there was, however, a fatal flaw in the life of Job. He had a deep problem, which we will discuss in the coming pages.

This chapter shares with us Job's financial and material worth, and his relationship to his family. We are shown an in-depth picture of Job as he relates to us his deep burden for his children. He offered burnt offerings on their behalf, that he might sanctify them in case they sinned and cursed God in their hearts. What a godly man! Yet you may wonder, "Brother Bonner, could a fatal flaw truly exist in this godly man?" Yes, and one did.

In *Job Chapter 1*, God allows us a glimpse into heaven. *Verse 6* begins by telling of the day the angels came before the Lord, and with them a visitor who had been given the right to come into the presence of God. He was the fallen angel, Lucifer, now known as Satan. At his appearing, the Lord asked Satan the question, "Where have you been?" Satan's response, in essence, was that he had been everywhere looking for one righteous, just, godly man. God then made the inquiry, "*Hast thou considered my servant, Job?*" and proceeded to list Job's good qualities, of which Satan was totally aware. The response of our enemy was, "Does Job fear God for naught?" Then we read on to find that Satan was not allowed to touch Job, which is incidentally, God's promise to every obedient Christian, for Satan goes on to say to God:

"You have made a hedge about him and about everything that he has and about all that he does, including not only the works of his hands, but his substance. But if you'll put forth your hand now and touch all he hath, he will curse thee to thy face."

Satan responded to God with this declaration because he felt he knew something about the true character of Job, and he did. So, God allowed the devil to move from that place into the presence of Job under the following conditions: All that he has is in your power, but don't you touch his flesh.

As the first chapter continues, we discover under God's guidelines, that Satan had come into the midst of all that Job owned, destroying it completely. This included a great wind from the wilderness that demolished the four corners of the house in which his children were socializing. It fell upon them and they were killed. Satan, with God's permission, had begun to "sift" the life of Job. Meanwhile, Job, upon hearing of each disastrous event, as his servants came to him and declared his losses, finally arose from where he was and, as was the custom to show deep brokenness, he rent his mantle or tore his clothes from his body. He shaved his head, perhaps with the sounds of a wailing mother and wife piercing his ears. He then fell down upon the ground, before God, and he worshipped.

FATAL FLAW

You say, "What a man of God!" Oh, yes! He was the most righteous man alive in the world at that time. The Scripture, however, says: "There is none righteous, no, not one." In fact, as we have already mentioned, Job had a fatal flaw. A consistent flaw in the life of a believer is referred to as a "stronghold". As we continue on to *Chapter 2* of the book of Job, we get a more developed picture of God's "best man," who "... *was perfect and upright*."

Chapter 2 begins by allowing us to look into heaven and, again, see a day when the sons of God came to present themselves before the Lord. Satan came also in the midst, for he stands as the "accuser of our brethren." God said to Satan, Where have you been? He essentially answered, "I have been looking for one righteous, just, and godly man." God's response to the adversary was:

> *"Hast thou considered my servant Job, that there is none like him in the earth, a perfect and an upright man, one that feareth God, and escheweth evil? and still he holdeth fast his integrity, although thou movest me against him, to destroy him without cause." (Job 2:3)*

Well, Brother Bonner, there it is. It's like a game, with God and Satan as the players, we as the pawns. For God stated that it was Satan who incited Him to move against Job, to prove to the devil that God's Word is immutable. My beloved, you will first see that Job had a fatal flaw. Secondly, you will discover the reason why God, who formed this angel in the beginning, cast him out of heaven and proved Himself and His Word to Satan. The devil had already experienced the omnipotent power of Almighty God. Yet Satan answered the Lord, *"Skin for skin, yea, all that a man hath will he give for his life. But put forth thine hand now, and touch his bone and his flesh, and he will curse thee to thy face."*

We saw in Chapter 1 that, because Job had obeyed God during his youth, God honored him, (*Job 29:4*). He must have tithed, resulting in God's blessing. He sacrificed to God. God, therefore, magnified his life. In fact, he met the criteria of all that was taught in that day about living and giving, and God esteemed him. We will scripturally address this later. In reference to Chapter 1, God permitted Satan to take from Job only his material and physical attributes, including the lives of his children. Then, a deeper level of brokenness occurred. God gave Satan permission to move against Job physically by stating, "**Behold, he is in thine hand; but save his life**." So, with permission to "touch his flesh", Satan went from the presence of the Lord and smote Job with sore boils, from the sole of his foot unto his crown. In other words, he put within him spirits of infirmity, (**Luke 13:11**).

Now, look at the response of this perfect man. He, in the midst of his brokenness, and in diminished health, began moving toward the ash pit of repentance. On the way, he picked up a piece of broken pottery and began to scrape the abscesses of his body to make his penance even more significant. With his flesh bleeding from the breaking of the boils, he sat down among the ashes in self-mortification. Satan, who felt he had Job in a defeated position, moved in to completely conquer his life. He brought Job's wife to him. She, desperate in heart over the loss of her children and fortune, saw the decaying state of her husband and accused him, saying, "**Doest thou still retain thine integrity?** (Do you still stand with God?) **Curse God and die**." The Scripture says she spoke as a "**foolish woman speaketh**," and Job's response to her was, "**What? Shall we receive good at the hand of God, and shall we not receive evil?**" In all of this Job did not sin with his lips.

You say, "Brother Bonner, what a man! What a man of God." Oh, yes, he was the finest that God had at that time. But as you will see, he had a fatal flaw. In his response to his wife, Job established that he knew exactly what was going on. He knew it was God who had allowed all that was happening in his life. In light of this, let's ask ourselves a question. If God, who is immutable, created and defeated Lucifer, and cast him and his angels to this ground, then who gave Satan the right to come back into God's Holy Presence with accusations? If God had the power to do all of this, was not His Word enough for our enemy?

Why would God put one of His children through all of this just to prove Himself to Satan?

Beloved, God has a plan and purpose in everything. I ask you now to take your eyes off of what seems to be an obvious teaching about Satan and focus your attention on the life and character of Job, based upon Job's own confessions, and of those of the Lord. We will further examine the declarations Job made of himself. He knew something was wrong in his own life.

To continue, we read in *Job 3:25* a statement coming from this man of God. It proves to be the truth in every case concerning God's discipline. He says, "*... for the thing which I greatly feared has come upon me, and that which I was afraid of has come unto me*." When you truly understand the depth of what he is saying, you will know that it is God alone who deals with His people in corrections, not Satan; for Satan has no power over the Christian without permission of God, being only God's messenger boy. *Hebrews 12:5-8* illustrates how God deals with believers:

> "*And ye have forgotten the exhortation which speaketh unto you as unto children, My son, despise not thou the chastening of the Lord, nor faint when thou are rebuked of Him: For whom the Lord loveth, He chasteneth, and scourgeth every son whom He receiveth. If ye endure chastening, God dealeth with you as with sons; for what son is he whom the Father chasteneth not? But if ye be without chastisement, whereof all are partakers, then are ye bastards, and not sons.*"

Based on these verses, we identify our loving Father's purpose in disciplining the believer. Look now at the circumstances of Job. He first encounters chastisement, the moving of God upon his circumstances. When there was no true repentance, scourging came, which is the moving of God upon the physical realm. In the first chapter, we discovered that Satan was allowed to proceed upon the peripheral life of Job. All of his children were slain and all that he owned was destroyed or taken. God dealt with Job from the classic position of chastisement, or the breaking of Job externally. In spite of the tragic losses recorded in *Chapter 1*, Job's fatal flaw was not corrected. So God, for the second time, allowed Satan to move upon him with scourging, which means that the body was attacked by satanic intervention, by spirits of infirmity, as a form discipline. Now, I know that many will reject this principle. But very often people later discover that they did not respond properly to God's discipline. Because they did not repent during the time of chastisement, scourging was allowed. Then, while lying upon their sick beds, they found pure repentance and the revelation of His Presence. This is the process of scourging as described in *Hebrews 12*. Scourging is the Greek word for "disease" or "plague" -- the moving upon the physical for rebuke and discipline.

In *Job 1 and 2*, we find this classic move of God which brought His children back into His Will. Incidentally, God says the evident sign that you are His child is this kind of disciplinary action in your life, in order to keep you functional as His elect. At the same time, it develops within you the character of the Person of Christ. God becomes sufficient to us only in our desperation. From that place, we learn the truth of His righteousness and adequacy, and we fall in love with Him. Please understand that no man will ever truly seek God with all his heart until he is emptied of the opportunities of working out his life in the flesh. From that emptied position, with utter desolation of life, he will move in abandonment toward God, through prayer, realizing God as his only hope. Then, God can supply not only the need, but His Life to that individual. What a joy to have Daddy (Abba) around when troubles come, for we are to cry "Abba - Father."

When my daughter Cynthia brought our first grandchild into the world, she experienced great labor. She was terrified. Even though I traveled constantly, I longed to be present when my baby bore her first child. When we finally arrived at the hospital, she wasn't crying for her husband, but for her dad. Then, when I prayed with her, she accepted the relationship again of her husband's place, but she said, "Oh, Daddy, I'm so glad you're here." How many times, in the process of breaking, have I been able to say, "Oh, Abba (Father, Daddy) (*Romans 8:15*), I'm so glad you're here." In my daughter's situation just the sound of my voice and knowing I was praying, gave her assurance. Thank God for prayer and the voice of God in our spirit. It is truly, blessed assurance.

Now, you say, "Brother Bonner, what are you doing to Mr. Job? Are you sure this is good theology?" Well, let's continue to *Job 7:17-21*. We must understand that prayer is God's power through man. Yet no man will ever be involved with God's Power until he is broken. Then, in that contrite state, through the cracks in his life, the Light of God will be emitted. Regarding brokenness, the writer of Job is inspired in *Chapter 7:17* to write: "*What is man that thou shouldest magnify him? and that thou shouldest set thine heart upon him?*" In other words, we are the vessels for God's Ministry just as Jesus was an extension of the Will of the Father. Constantly isolating Himself for the purpose of prayer, He sought after God's mind. We too, through prayer, are to seek the Will of the Father as His Kingdom comes and His Will is done on earth as it is in heaven.

In *Verse 18*, God tells us that He visits us every morning. That's why it is so essential that you, as a Christian, upon awakening each day, pray the prayer: "Father, in the name of Jesus Christ, I give you my life today," and then stay in praise until He has said "yes" to your spirit, (*Jeremiah 33:3, Ephesians 3:16*). What a day that will be! (*Psalms 118:24*)

Continuing in these verses, Job cried out to God, "*How long wilt thou not depart from me, nor let me alone till I swallow down my spittle?*" or, in essence, "Why, God, are you doing this to me?" So, in this state of being, what did he do? He made an effort to repent. *Verse 20* says:

> "*I have sinned; what shall I do unto thee, O thou preserver of men? why hast thou set me as a mark against thee, so that I am a burden to myself?*"

Finally, in the *21st verse*, he asked God why this forgiveness had not come:

> "*Why doest thou not pardon my transgression, and take away my iniquity? for now I shall sleep in the dust; and thou shalt seek me in the morning, but I shall not be.*"

Or, better said, "Oh, God, end all this misery, let me die."

You say, "At last he is broken. He's crying out to God, and in the midst of his entreaty, he has finally repented." Yes, by his standard, he repented, but did God accept it? No. Why not? Because it was not true repentance. True repentance comes only through the door of true brokenness, (*Psalm 51:17*). You must see what God sees to be truly repentant.

Now, hold that thought and let's take a further look at Job and see what was really inside of him. Chapter 19 shows us a man who cried out for understanding from his friends. When this scourging first occurred in Job's life, his friends came and sat for seven days, mourning with him, without speaking a word. Then, suddenly, conversation broke out and, in the course of it, reasoning crept in through the door of accusation, as Job's friends tried to find out why he was going through this crisis. Surely he had done something wrong! I believe Satan was behind their accusations, and was desperately attempting to get Job to break, (**Revelation 12:10**). God, however, knowing His man even deeper, allowed this crisis to bring Job to the place of seeing himself as he really was. In this chapter, it is evident that God had conceded to even greater pressure upon Job, as Satan continued to sift him. Job was the target of strong disapproval as his friends lamented a man who, at one time, was very likely the wealthiest in the world. But Job sat poverty-stricken and in broken health. "Why?" they asked themselves. Soon, the condemnations began to fly.

You see, we are now coming face to face with Job's dark area, for the real character of a person always surfaces at tribulation. For instance, he looked to his friends, in the 21st verse, and cried out:

> *"Have pity upon me, have pity upon me, O ye my friends; for the hand of God hath touched me. Why do you persecute me as God, and are not satisfied with my flesh?"*

Here we get a true picture of these friends, as well as an insight of Job's problem. They, very likely for years, had been jealous of what God had done to and through this man. They resented the overwhelming presence of honor God gave to Job because of his commitment to God during the years as a youth. For that, he was mightily blessed. Job's friends saw their opportunity to discredit Job. Something had happened between

God and Job. You must understand that many of their accusations about Job's life were correct, but they were handled in the wrong spirit. We now begin to see the true light of this relationship. Men who had held him in fear, esteem, and great honor, because of his great wealth, are now persecuting him. Jealousy is one of Satan's strongest allies to the soul or flesh of man. I believe this was hidden in their hearts all the time. Incidentally, one of the things in these two verses that we must not turn our back upon is the fact that, again, Satan is God's messenger boy, and through all of this experience, Job still knew that it was God who was dealing with him. He greatly feared and "*knew,*" (*Job 3:25*).

FAMOUS IN UZ

As we continue through the book of Job, we now come to his character flaw. Please remember that all God had to do was say to Satan, "Job is totally righteous." For His Word is sovereign and eternal. It is paramount. God, however, could not say this about Job because Christians are only as righteous as they allow God to be righteous in them. The believer's righteousness is based on the level of control given to God, as a result of individual yieldedness to the Holy Spirit, (*Romans 3:10*).

Righteousness can be measured only in the Person of Christ, not in the religious position of man. In fact, we find Job's true character in *Chapter 29*. Here we see what was really inside the best that God had on the earth. In this chapter, Job, under the pressure of pride, continued to explain who and where he was in life before his tragedy befell. This could best be summarized as his lamentation. In these verses, we find that he used the words "I," "my," and "me" to defend himself thirty-nine times, according to the translation. In fact, in the entire book, these personal references to himself are used three-hundred thirty-three times. In these defensive declarations of his self-worth lies the true description of spirituality. You see, all the wonderful blessings given to Job in his younger life, before his judgment, were bestowed because of his complete love, commitment, and obedience to God.

From that posture of submission and reverence to the teaching of the Word, as it was in that day, and knowing that all that had happened to him was by the Power of God, the Father continued to honor him by increasing what he possessed. Soon he became famous for the blessings of God upon his life. This is one of the most dangerous aspects of God's prosperity as He promises He will do in His Word. If an individual is not strong in memory, he will soon begin to turn the accolades inward. The first seeds of pride are always planted in the field of rebellion, a wanting to take authority. In Job's case, somewhere along the line Satan told him how good he was and he began to assume responsibility for all the blessings. Pride is the greatest enemy of the soul, in that when pride is sown in the soil of egoism it begins to germinate. The enemy whispers, "Look at what I am doing." The individual, like Job, forgets his origin, and finally adopts an improper co-identity with God. Soon, he attempts to assume some of God's Glory, sharing with God His Harvest and its blessings.

Satan, knowing our weaknesses, whispers to our minds, "Without you, God could not have..." and then, "If it were not for your ability, where would God be in these matters? Your judgment in what you do is as good as His. Why pray?" From there, it is all down hill. Again, pride is the soul's greatest enemy. Job had become famous in Uz for who he was and for how God's blessings were abundantly upon him. Job's flesh was weak, and as the honors came, he began to listen with his soul (flesh). He became known as "God's man," and through Satan's wiles to destroy (*Ephesians 6:11*), there began within him a sharing of all that God had done. How true the Scripture of *Matthew 19:23*, that teaches that it is hard for a rich man to enter into the kingdom of heaven! We must remember that the Christian life is one of transformation and transferal. We become less as He becomes more, and God ministers through us and is sovereignly honored, (*II Corinthians 3:5*).

Someone once said, "What do you get when you squeeze a lemon?" The answer is not just lemon juice, but what's inside. When Job became more and more known for his wealth and ability, he began to share, in his own heart, the glory that should have been given solely to God, (*Daniel 5:20*). Having been squeezed by his friends, who had no longer given him a place of respect and honor, Job found himself under the real pressure of pride. He declared to his friends, in defense of his own person, "See what I have done!" It all goes along with his statement, "Pity me, pity me." In explanation of his personal service to mankind in *29:2-3*, he talks of being preserved of God, as he declares "***When His candle shined upon my head ...***" as he walked in the light of God. In fact, before the Christian is broken, he explains his ministry as "Me" or "Mine." Then, as breaking begins, and revelation into his life is being illuminated, his statement becomes, "Me and God." As he continues in brokenness, his explanation develops to "God and Me." But, when he finally matures in brokenness, his ministry is defined as being "God, All God." Oh, how wonderful the place!

Samuel Pearse was called the "Brainerd of the Baptists" and did much to forward the missionary enterprise of William Carey in India by faithfully "holding the ropes" at home. Later, his daughter married one of Dr. Carey's sons. Pearse was aware of his danger of spiritual pride as was recorded by his biographer: "I am ashamed," he writes to Ryland, "that I have so much pride. I want more and more to become a little child, to dwindle into nothing in my esteem, to renounce my own wisdom, power, and goodness, and to simply live upon Jesus for all."

In a letter to his wife from Plymouth, he sadly confesses: "My thirst for preaching Christ, I fear abates; and a detestable vanity for the reputation of a good preacher, as the world terms it, has already cost me many conflicts..." He wrote to Carey: "Flattering prospects of reputation and wealth have too much ascendancy over me. "

Continuing on in Job's defense of his own righteousness, he told his friends about his personal abilities. He declared that it all began, "In the days of my youth." Here lies the real truth of his success, as he professed, "*... when the secret of God was upon my tabernacle,*" (*Job 29:4*). Once more, in his early days, he was completely and absolutely committed daily to God. Job had, with extreme effort, brought his life into a complete submission of all of God's principles that he had been taught. He deeply loved God and it is evident that he stood in reverential awe of his Lord. In that kind of equation, God always brings His Life to and through the individual. Oh, the blessing of having been totally submitted and yielded to God as his Sovereign! In fact, he expressed it: "When God was upon my tabernacle, the rock poured me out rivers of oil." How wonderful his youthful experience with God! Do you remember when you were first born again, how you practiced the wonders of His grace? It is well said, "As long as you're green, you will grow. It is when you get ripe that you get rotten."

Job, during his youth, was in complete submission to the Father, thereby producing the Presence and Will of God through his life. As a result, great honor was brought to him as men attributed the blessings he received to his obedience to the Lord. However, in the midst of Job's "God blessed lifestyle," (as observed in others who have made this trip), there was the constant fighting of his own pride to let God instruct him. He was quick to give God the glory for all that had happened to him. He knew it was God and he praised Him.

This entire scenario has been played out before. In the annals of time, Jesus created the highest of all angels and called his name Lucifer, "son of the morning," "bright and shining one." According to *Ezekiel 28*, Lucifer was designed by Christ to "seal up the sum." This meant that Lucifer was not only full of wisdom, but was also "perfect in beauty." When Christ made him, He had prepared within Lucifer's throat a musical instrument to lead the chorus of angels in anthems of praise before the presence of the throne. The Scripture calls these "tabarets" and "viols." This gloriously created being, however, one day noticed the high regard given him by the other angels. He observed how he "*was the full measure and pattern of exactness,*" (*Ezekiel 28:12 Amplified*). He saw that his intelligence was far beyond the other angels and enjoyed how they stood in his presence almost in awe. Suddenly, welling up inside of him was the thought not of what he was, or his origin and creation, but who he could be. Then, in total submission to his own thoughts, he finally and fatally declared in *Isaiah 14:13-14*, the true position of pride: "*I will.*" In fact, these verses state that he declared, "*I will ascend above the heights of the clouds: I will be like the most High.*" Therefore, pride had its origin in this, a created angelic being. He disregarded that he was an instrument of God's Glory. Pride consumed and destroyed him. He lost his first estate and was cast out of heaven.

As I look across the many years of my ministry, I can recall the names of great men of God whose skills were far beyond the normal and natural. These were ministers whose oratorical abilities were significantly above and beyond that of the average; many of whose writings would search out the Spirit and place on paper the Mind of God so uniquely that it would change, as it did mine, the hearts of the readers. Their early youthful beginnings were in complete submission to God, with daily prayer and Bible study. As the applause came, however, their first love faded. They took for themselves the glory of what God had done through their lives, only then to leave the ministry or sink into oblivion, fruitless and in shame. God will not share His honor or His Glory.

R. A. Torrey said, "Oh, how many a man has been full of promise and God has used him, and then that man thought that he was the whole thing and God was compelled to set him aside! I believe more promising workers have gone on the rocks through self-sufficiency and self-esteem than through any other cause.

I can look back for forty years, or more, and think of many men who are now wrecks or derelicts who, at one time, were thought by the world to be something great. But they have disappeared entirely from public view. Why? Because of over-estimation of self."

Here is a poem that expresses this tragedy:

> I knew a youth of large and lofty soul,
> A soul aflame with heavenly purpose high;
> Like a young eagle's, his clear, earnest eye,
> Fixed on the sun, could choose no lesser goal.
> For truth he lived; and love, a burning coal,
> From God's high altar, did the fire supply,
> That flushed his cheeks as morning tints the sky,
> And kept him pure by its Divine control.

Lately, I saw him, smooth and prosperous,
Of portly presence and distinguished air.
The cynic's smile of self-content was there,
The very air about him breathed success.
Yet, by the eyes of love, too plainly seen,
Appeared the wreck of what might have been.

Unknown

We must be broken to be used.

THE GOLDEN RULE IS,
"HE WHO HAS THE GOLD, RULES"

Continuing in *Job 29*, we read that Job began to talk about how the "seats of honor" were prepared for him, and how the "young men hid themselves" and "the aged stood up in his presence." Even princes would refrain from speaking when he came on the scene. With all this attention, it is evident that he began to lose sight of the fact that God had been his source, forgetting that he had simply allowed God to extend Himself through him. This extension of God in an individual is because of servanthood and submission in prayer. Finally, Job did succumb to the applause, the constant homage, the patting on the back, and to the declaration that "when the ear heard <u>him</u>, it blessed <u>him</u>, and when the eye saw <u>him</u>, it gave witness to <u>him</u>," (*Chapter 29:11*). Perhaps, somewhere along the way, he quit insisting to those around him, "Oh, it's God. Please understand, it's all God." As bad as I hate to admit it, many, many times after great victory in my personal ministry I too have forgotten to whom the glory is due. God forgive me. It is lonely drawing attention to yourself as the Presence of God backs away from your spirit. It is a spiral downward.

In Job's life, the position of "I" and "self" began to surface as he spoke further about his abilities and what he had accomplished. In his own defense, he explained how he helped the poor, and how the fatherless were given things by him. Soon, people had begun to exalt him. As the old adage says, "he who has the gold, rules." Job perhaps became possessed by his possessions, and felt that it was he who personally helped those who "were ready to perish." He "caused the widow's heart to sing for joy." In fact, he declared, "I put on righteousness and it clothed me." Then, in trying to convince his friends of his personal achievements, he stated, "*My judgment was as a robe and a diadem*." What a declaration! Job felt "he was eyes to the blind, feet to the lame, and father to the poor!" He thought it was himself who "*brake the jaws of the wicked and plucked the spoil out of his teeth*."

As a result of the great pressure of being squeezed and accused, Job's fatal flaw was made evident. He believed that the glory was freshly upon him when he declared, "I will do." He repeatedly confessed that his righteousness was a direct result of "I," "My," or "Me." It is evident that in Job's mind, he believed that his ability, coupled with God's Power, made a great team. In fact, he probably reached the conclusion that "God and I (not God through me) can do anything." What a partnership. In spite of Job's growing pride, the world most likely continued to recognize only Job's abilities. (Satan saw to that.) To top it all off, Satan knew that Job was growing in "self." Again, it must be understood that God shares His Glory with no one. We are vessels of His Honor and of His Glory. In light of this, there have been only a few men in history, who, blessed by God's Ministry through them, could keep what was happening in proper perspective . They were not consumed by what God had given them to give away to others in His Name.

Much is said about pride, especially in the book of Proverbs. Job experienced a transition in his life, beginning in his youth, when he heard from God, and continued through the path of pride. The results of this disaster are expressed to us in **Proverbs 8:13**, which says, "**The fear of the Lord is to hate evil: pride, and arrogancy, and the evil way, and the froward mouth do I hate**." Again, He says in **Proverbs 11:2**, "**When pride cometh, then cometh shame: but with the lowly is wisdom**." Then, in **Proverbs 13:10**, he says, "**Only by pride cometh contention: but with the well-advised is wisdom**." Also, in **Proverbs 14:3**, "**In the mouth of the foolish is a rod of pride: but the lips of the wise shall preserve them**."

But, oh, there exists a declarative verse that has been the trapdoor to millions of Christians, who have forgotten from where the blessings have come. They have walked from the brilliancy of the room of revelation to the long corridor of self, and into the darkness of vain glory, falling into Satan's pit, (**Psalms 35:7**). God says in **Proverbs 16:18**, "**Pride goeth before destruction, and a haughty spirit before a fall**." As we have and will further see, this eloquently describes Job's journey. Before we leave Proverbs, please note another essential verse: "**A man's pride shall bring him low: but honour shall uphold the <u>humble</u> <u>in</u> <u>spirit</u>**," (**Proverbs 29:23**). Someone well said, "All desire to be humble, but few desire to be humbled."

Edwin Harvey tells of a translation of a certain book that was sent to J. N. Darby by its author. In the preface, the writer had given a most flattering opinion of the eminence and piety of J. N. Darby. We give, in abbreviated form, the letter Darby sent to the author, in which he repudiated the undue praise:

"Pride is the greatest of all evils that beset us, and of all our enemies, it is that which dies the slowest and hardest; even the children of the world are able to discern this. Madam de Stael said on her deathbed, 'Do you know what is the last to die in man? It is self-love'."

"God hates pride above all things," Darby continues, "because it gives to man the place that belongs to Him who is above, exalted overall. Pride intercepts communion with God, and draws down His chastisement, for 'God resisteth the proud'."

Job had gone as low as one could go, resulting in his own desire for death. He lost everything. He faced the abandonment of those who respected him. He experienced the loss of physical health. Not only was there total destruction of what he had and was, but he believed that all was lost, and gone forever. Gone but not forgotten. But worst of all, gone. The real tragedy in Job's life, despite all of his "losses," was that he still did not understand why he faced these catastrophic circumstances.

Before we go any further in this writing, it must be understood that the Book of Job is not only about patience, but repentance. The name Job itself is derived from an Arabic word signifying repentance. In light of this, let us see how God dealt with the sin of His finest man.

HERE COMES THE JUDGE

God, our Righteous Judge, is always on the scene, (**Hebrews 13:5**). One way or another in the believer's life, He will speak to the spirit man, revealing to him the evil within his heart, and the explanation of His judgment. You must remember that this manuscript is about brokenness. At the beginning of this book, I quoted Job as saying, "***The thing I*** *greatly feared is come upon me*." God had dealt with Job, first of all, by conviction within his inner man. Secondly, Job experienced the Hand of God upon his outer man, as we find now in *Chapter 38*.

Incidentally, one of the classic prayer verses in the Bible is *Job 37:19*. It states, "*Teach us what we shall say unto Him; for we cannot order our speech by reason of darkness*." Another way to say it is, "**We know not what we should pray for as we ought, but the Spirit itself maketh intercession for us with groanings that cannot be uttered**," (*Romans 8:26*). We must know the Mind of God in prayer and agree with it because the Scripture states, "*Thy Kingdom come, Thy Will be done, on earth as it is in heaven*," (*Matthew 6:10*). His Will is already working in us if we are able to hear and obey, (*Ephesians 2:10*).

As we continue, the scene changes radically. We read that Job sat in a pile of ashes, facing the men who tried to discern his sins. Suddenly, there was a whirlwind. As it passed closely by Job, the wind's sound became the Voice of God. Here, a classic question is asked of Job by his Creator: "*Who is this that darkeneth counsel by words without knowledge?*" In other words, God told Job that he (Job) had no concept of what was really happening to him. Then He demanded Job to, "*gird up now thy loins like a man*." In other words, "Shut up and listen for I am about to tell you your real problem." He began by putting Job in his proper perspective, in order to restore him. This is the purpose of brokenness: to see in our lives what God sees.

As He questioned Job, we are able to understand God's position concerning Job's lordship over his own life. God asks, "*Where wast thou when I laid the foundations of the earth? declare, if thou has understanding*."

Needless to say, God had Job's complete attention, for as He came into the presence of a confused man, one who had forgotten the origins of the joys that he experienced and was now taking credit for the ministry of God through him. He was commanded of God to listen. Again, tribulation is God's way of clearing the air, and while in its midst, we can see what is truly happening. Then God declared to Job, in essence, "I don't remember seeing you when I made the world." In other words, God said to him, "In what you have done, you were trying to become co-equal with me. I am God alone. In fact, you were not even around when I made the world." His point was that He can use only the vessel of a committed individual who will yield to Him all of his life that He (God), through him, can minister His Will and receive Glory to His Name. Someone has said, "God does not need our ability, but our availability," or perhaps stated God's way, "I don't need any help."

Remember, again, Job's statement about himself as a youth in *Chapter 29*. We see in the beginning a dedicated, committed young man, who brought honor to God with his life. God took that vessel and extended His Glory through it. But then came the fight of the flesh. Satan, having trapped him, knew Job for what he really was. Job was, as all are, "conceived in sin." This is why, I believe, when the devil made his deal with God regarding Job's life, he knew what was really hidden within him. "You deny him and he'll curse you to your face," Satan said to God. The devil understood, that through pride, he had captured him in his fleshly state. Job had the fatal human flaw.

THE BEGINNING OF THE END

Now, let's look at what happens when a Christian is placed first into chastisement and later into scourging. If the believer responds correctly to this confrontation, he will, in repentance, yield his life back to God. He will become broken over his sin and will cry out for forgiveness and restoration. David stated it best before his fall in *Psalm 34:18, "The Lord is nigh unto them who are of a broken heart and saveth such as be of a contrite spirit*." Then, after the great disaster and judgment upon David's life because of his immoral relationship with Bathsheba, he cried out from a vanquished position, "*The sacrifices of God are a broken spirit: a broken and a contrite heart, O God, thou will not despise,*" (*Psalm 51:17*).

Such was Job in this encounter, when God came into his presence in the whirlwind. Always, from the position of tribulation, do we see in the light of His Glory, the darkness of the sin of our own lives. As the light of God's Glory was shown upon the darkness of Job's sin, he saw himself truly as he was. He was devastated, broken, and contrite. Brokenness always occurs when God comes upon the scene in revival or prayer. People are broken. As God continued with his questioning in the 38th and 39th chapters, Job was totally exposed before his Sovereign Holy Father and was stripped of all self in the "*terror of his soul,*" (*Job 31:23*). In the encounter, his self-righteousness exploded before his eyes as he was then in the presence of pure Righteousness. The Light of God was revealed to Job when the mirror of his life became darkened with pride, and his reflection before men was no longer of God.

Finally, in *Chapter 40*, God continued His vocal surgery of Job with this classic, eternal line in the second verse:

"Shall he that contendeth with the Almighty instruct him? he that reproveth God, let him answer it."

God's message to Job was, "Somewhere in the midst of this transition of My Life through you, by your choice, We became co-equal in the work. You decided to minister according to the dictates of your own personal heart, instead of My blessing Myself through you. You are now in a contest with Me. You are now saying that I cannot conduct My business according to My Will so, you are reproving Me and taking over your life, and also taking the glory for the work I have done through you."

Elizabeth Forster wrote, "Human nature always seeks its own, sets a value upon itself, wills to be self-dependent, and measures all others by its over-valued self. No wonder then that *'He was despised and rejected of men'* ..."

Many times I have personally taken control of my ministry. I have interrupted the beginning growth of God's Will in my life, and grafted into its roots my own direction for evangelism, which always produced illegitimate fruit. I only found myself in the lonely place of separation from God's Will. I have, over and over, begged God to forgive me. In the failure of my efforts or works without God, He would, in essence, say to me, "You're in a contest with me. In other words, you are trying to reprove or improve on what I want to do through you." Beloved friend, it just won't work. How I have failed God in so many endeavors! I was zealous, but wrong, (**Romans 10:2-3**).

How often in tribulation has God brought us back into His Will only to re-establish that which He desires to do through us? Thank God for blessed brokenness that births obedience!

No one can truly see himself as he is until, in the experience of brokenness, he is driven back into the Presence of God in true prayer. An example of this is evident as God came on the scene in the Book of Job. The Light of His Presence shone in the darkness of Job's soul, and he saw for himself what God already knew about him. Within this realm lies the birth of all true ministry. It is the beginning of all breaking. As a result of this entire process, Job acquired a new language, reflected in *Job 40:3 5*.

> "*Job answered the Lord and said, 'Behold, I am vile; what shall I answer thee? I will lay my hand upon my mouth. Once I have spoken; but I will not answer: yea, twice; but I will proceed no further'.*"

Herein are the classic steps to brokenness as they were birthed in Job's life.

STOP THE WORLD, I WANT TO GET OFF

What happens to your life when God, through brokenness or blessing, truly reveals Himself? First of all, you see yourself as God sees you. Never had this kind of language burst forth from the mouth of Job. The presence of God and desperate conviction brought Job to that point. From the depths of his soul came the cry, "*Behold, I am vile.*" You who are students of this book will remember how in *Job 23:1-8* he stated that he would fill his mouth with arguments if God would only come to him and give him a fair trial. He was maintaining in those verses that he would like to talk to God and explain his problems. In these verses, Job, in essence, said: "Come here and let me plead my case to you. If you could only truly see me as I am."

What was his reaction, however, when God did come into his presence? As in every case, he saw himself as he really was.

Beloved, to be used of God we must see ourselves as He sees us. We cannot truly deal with human sickness until there is the proper diagnosis of the ailment. When that comes, medicines can be given to the body to overcome its malady, unless, by prayer, there is a level of faith to stand against it for healing. But, in this case, Job cried out, "*Behold, I am vile.*" This is a completely different language from the man who was held in such high esteem for so long, not only by himself, but by others around him. Yet, this will always be the result when we truly see what God sees in our lives. We will be broken over our sins. And to ever be used of God, brokenness is the imperative. No individual will ever see God's working through his life without it.

From the explosion of Light in Job's dark soul, we are given by God an insight into the greatest stronghold in the life of the believer, and how it enters in. He said, "*What shall I answer thee? I will lay mine hand upon my mouth.*" How many of you, when you suddenly lost your victorious walk with God, asked, "God, what did I do?" In reality, it was not what you did, but it was what you said. Satan, for the most part, enters the life of the Christian through his mouth. For the Bible says:

> "*Not that which goeth into the mouth defileth a man; but that which cometh out of the mouth, this defileth a man,*" (Matthew 15:11).

Satan's ministry is to divide. He accomplishes this when you react negatively or angrily at some scenario. His demons, because of your lack of prayer or praise, come in like a flood. When Job saw himself through God, and realized that his problem was his confession, he stated, "*I will lay mine hand upon my mouth. Once I have spoken; yea, twice; but I will not proceed no further.*"

In the light of this, let's see Job's reaction to God's Presence. In his broken state, after having come face to face with God in the whirlwind, he turned the corner with his life, for he then declared, "I WILL PROCEED NO FURTHER." Now, did this mean that he was going to die? In a sense, yes. Job had decided with all of his heart, having come into the Presence of God, that he would experience from an Old Testament position that which we experience in the New, that of being *crucified with Christ*" as read in *Galatians 2:20*. The Christian will experience no greater event than that of coming to the end of himself. This will begin the Ministry of Christ through him. When Christians cease to be partakers of the world's carnality, God will initiate a deep work.

From that place, the Holy Spirit begins to work out Christ's Ministry through the believer. Again, "*I am crucified with Christ,*" is the declaration of *Galatians 2:20*. There is an old saying, "Dead men tell no tales." By the same token, dead men take no credit. God, therefore, can perform His Will through them. My beloved, if we could learn to yield our lives to God, with the dynamics of His Will driving us to Him with all that we are, then He could begin, through us, to extend the purpose and plan for our lives as written in heaven, (*Ephesians 2:10*). We would come to a place of victory and joy unspeakable, such as we've never known. We would cease to be masters and begin to be servants. Oh, the wondrous joy of the transformed life! "It is joy unspeakable and full of glory," (*I Peter 1:8*).

Elizabeth Forster expressed it well when she wrote: "Men cannot understand a hidden life. They press every advantage to make as much of themselves as they can. But here is something more than modesty in Jesus; He hid His face that He might manifest His Father's; He sank into insignificance that He might be the express Image of His Father, so serving His

Purpose in everything. This is the way of the cross for us as for our Master.

The way of the cross not only saves man from hell, but also crosses him out, to write the name of Jesus Christ in the place of his; Christ hides man and manifests God."

We are taking this lengthy trip through this wonderful book to establish the position of brokenness. As I said before, every true ministry that is sovereign of God has had its birth in the Cross. So much is done today by man's physical effort, in the name of Christ, with greatly desired hope that He will join the manipulation with His manifestation. However, it does not work that way. Our works without His Will are dead efforts or flesh. They are "wood, hay, stubble."

Until we have experienced brokenness to the degree that God is our only sufficiency in the matter, there will never be a pure work of grace. This work of grace was made manifest in Job's youth when he became aware of Godly Truth and exercised it by faith. Because of Job's faithfulness, God poured out His Glory on everything he touched. But, as in every case, when pride entered in, things began to happen to Job. He became known for who he was, (master), rather than for whom he represented, (servant), or, in reality, the extension of the Will of God. Again, it is a rare occurrence when one so blessed of God does not hear the whispers of Satan through the mouths of men, to not only take credit for the endeavor, but to begin to take over and minister by their own personal direction rather than, through prayer, seeking the Will of God.

William Cowper penned:

"Beware of too sublime a sense
Of your own worth and consequence.
The man who dreams himself so great,

And his importance of such weight,
That all around in all that's done,
Must move and act for him alone,
Will learn in school of tribulation,
The folly of his expectation ..."

PAY DAY

Pride is the building that burns to the ground when the fires of God come through tribulation. For pride is dead tender. It is only from these ashes that a foundation can be established that is "laid by Christ Jesus." Oh, how blessed is brokenness, and the wonderful experiences of joy that materialize within its crucible! Thus it was with Job, whose material wealth rose through the edifice of faith.

Then, in later life, he discovered its foundations crumbling, for it was structured in the sands of pride, rather than upon the Rock. Rare is the circumstance when a man so blessed of God can win the battle of self-righteousness without losing his place in grace or, better said, takes over what God has blessed him with. Perhaps it could be stated in another way -- it takes him over. Job's encounter with God in the whirlwind had caused him to see himself as he really was. This confrontation became a greater crisis to him than the loss of what he had and the loss of his health. Such was the experience of one whose circumstances had come face to face with the revelation of the Holy Spirit. He had a desperate conviction of sin. The Will of God is birthed in an individual's life at the moment of complete contriteness. As for Job, the reward of brokenness finally arrived. While in the presence of God, Job was shattered, and in his grief-stricken, sorrowful state, he was transformed. He realized that trying to convince his friends of his own righteousness was vain.   Turned inward, and in hopeless despair, he cried out, "*I WILL PROCEED NO FURTHER*." Beloved, true ministry begins as you turn from the "*I will*" of Satan's pride position (*Isaiah 14:12-14*) to the "*I Am*" of God's complete control over all things, (*Genesis 3:14*).   All must experience it to go on with God. It is the imperative.

CHILDREN OF PRIDE

Job 40-41 exemplifies the discipline of God as He questions Job.   It appears seemingly impossible for Job to answer the Lord at this point. So, God told him of an animal that is king over all. He spoke of its size, power, authority, and dominance, and declared that it cannot be controlled. In this Old Testament parable of the Leviathan, God explained Job's problem. Such is the mind of the Father. For Job realized what He was talking about in that God stated in *41:34*, "*He beholdeth all high things: he is a king (monarch) over all the children of pride*."   Of course, this meant that as the Leviathan was the literal king of all the animals, Satan was/is king over the proud, able to manipulate and control lives. Thus was Job, until God came on the scene. Always remember that Satan operates in darkness; God operates in light. Job could not see his sin because of "*reason of darkness*," (*Job 37:19*).

The Scripture also teaches, in *Psalm 73:6*:

"Therefore pride comepasseth them about as a chain; violence covereth them as a garment."

Proverbs 8:13 teaches:

> *"The fear of the Lord is to hate evil: pride, and arrogancy, and the evil way, and the froward mouth, do I hate."*

From these truths, we find that Job had traded places with God, allowing Satan to set him up. Satan knew that he had created within Job's life an attitude of, "Look what I'm doing for God. Look how the world honors me." Job himself stated, "*I put on righteousness (moral) and it clothed me, my judgment (divine law) as a robe and a diadem.*" Or, in essence, "I am like God." Pride. God, however, knew the real heart of His man and that in the situation of tribulation and breaking Job would choose against his personal will and be birthed again into truth and righteousness. The same is true of every person who desperately wants to go on with God. We must, with all of our hearts, come to the cross, and from there allow God to begin His Ministry through us. Please understand we do not build a true work of God by going toward the cross (flesh or religion), but by living from the cross, (brokenness through crucifixion). Because Job's perspective had become distorted, God permitted Satan to "sift him as wheat," in order to restore Job to God's Ministry and Will.

Now, let's look at the results of his breaking and what I believe is the real message of this book. Please keep in mind that the name "Job" means "repentance" in Arabic. In Chapter *42:1-2*, Job admitted the total sovereignty of God. Even the thoughts of his mind were registered into the knowledge of God. Earlier, however, he tried to get God on the scene to inform Him of his own righteousness. Please remember that all through the fabric of this journal is woven the thread of conviction as he continued to say over and over that it was God that had brought this discipline to him. Read again as Job declares, "*The thing I greatly feared has come upon me.*"

Beloved, you must understand that God will not put Christians into tribulation without first making them aware that something is desperately wrong in their hearts. This is explained in *Job 42:3*. The sovereignty of God and the consciousness of His Glory must be consummated in the innermost being, or truth will not be ministered. Profound truth is ministered only through brokenness. In the light of this, Job asserted:

> "*Who is he that hideth counsel without knowledge? therefore have I uttered that I understood not; things too wonderful for me, which I knew not.*"

Job knew about God, but he did not know God. Our churches are filled today with people who have a knowledge of God, (knosis), but no revelation of Him, (epiknosis), or higher knowledge. They have never experienced His real Presence or Glory in their personal lives other than the moment of their Salvation. For it must be grasped that true comprehension of God and His triumph comes to the spirit of man only by revelation of the Holy Spirit. Most men today do not essentially want God's Will or direction. As the old saying goes, "I would rather do it myself." Pride, plus the world's satanic dominion, plus demonic intrusion, equals constant confusion and powerless ministry. Another way to say it is, "Let's design a program and ask God to bless it." People, therefore, find themselves in ministry doing good and godly things void of His Power. Confusion! From this point of view, Job uttered, spoke, and experienced the truths of God by what he had been taught in his youth. Even so, he never understood them. My beloved friend, if ever a verse should spark our hearts to the reality of righteousness and to a walk of faith, it should be this one. Job, man of God, blessed of God, made formidable by God, became conscious of what was happening and began to share in its glory. Again, Job's fatal flaw was the same as Satan's -- the one who sought to overcome him. Pride!

THIS TOO SHALL PASS

During the Roman Empire, when a general would return to Rome with his victorious army after a great conquest of battle, he would also bring the spoils of war. The whole population would attend his parade to see the officers of the defeated army chained to his chariot, being dragged from behind. The people would then cheer his triumph! To be received in true glory as an able commander must have been the experience of a lifetime. Their cries were, "Hail the conquering hero!" However, lest his worth be overwhelming in his own mind, it was a custom of that nation to also have in that garland draped chariot of war, a servant who, for the entire parade, stood behind him whispering in the great hero's ear: "This too shall pass." What a statement! Please understand that when you take the victory for what God has done through you, you also have received the fullness of your reward. But when you give God all of the glory for His work through you, your reward is eternal. An old adage states, "Only one life will soon be passed; only what's done for (by) Christ will last." This is the gold, refined by fire, spoken of in the Scripture.

Dear friend, what a joy it would be if you began praying today to be broken, knowing that you can trust your Heavenly Father to take care of you in the midst of any trial! Remember, any circumstance you might face would be used by God to accomplish His Purpose in you. God would reveal to you the status of your relationship with Him. Having seen yourself through the Cross, you could say as Job did, "Oh, God, I know the 'why' of these wonderful breakings now. You are all and all in my life. You are sufficient in these matters. I truly love you. I praise your name. Praise the Lord."

When you become submitted and obedient in your breaking through praise, God explodes within you the joy of His true person and you now know a living, Holy, Sovereign God, (*Philippians 3:10*). This is illustrated to us in the third verse of *Job 42.* Here, broken before God, Job's spirit man cried out, "*Things too wonderful for me which I knew not.*" In essence, Job experienced God in his heart and was overwhelmed with joy. The encounter led Job to see God in his spirit. As a result, he saw himself. His eyes were finally opened.

Now, beloved, please listen with your hearts to what Job then begged God to do. He cried, in the fourth and fifth verses:

"*Hear, I beseech thee, and I will speak: I will demand of thee, and declare thou unto me. I have heard of thee by the hearing of the ear: but now mine eye seeth thee.*"

What is he saying? Upon having seen God, he saw himself, and was totally devastated over his sinful, prideful life. He was, in the confrontation, contrite (crushed), and he turned his life back to God in complete abandonment. This was evidenced when he begged the Lord to take complete control of his being. Notice the change in his language. Instead of getting his friends to understand how righteous he was, he was now crying directly to God, "Please, oh, please, I beg you to hear, Father, what I am saying to you." Then he used the words "I demand."

Job's words indicate to us that he might have declined to the place of taking authority over God's Will. But this is not the case. Job was actually begging, "Please, oh God, please, give Yourself to me. I want You more than anything else in this world. I must have You. You must take over my life. You must control my heart and my being from this moment on. Please, oh please, oh Father, please, fill me with Your life. Be the Lord of my life. You must. YOU MUST!"

In principle, this is the purpose of all brokenness. It reveals the wondrous person of Jesus Christ to the "hidden man of the heart" that He, through him, might extend His Will and carry on life the work of the Holy Spirit.

Beloved, as you're reading this, I want you to look back in your Christian walk and remember the greatest moments of grace that you have had with God. Think of the times when His Presence was so overwhelming that joy flooded your soul and peace consumed you. Even in the midst of the trials you were facing at that time, you accomplished a rest in the Lord with *"joy unspeakable and full of glory."* Has that ever happened to you? Then take one more step back in your memory to the test that brought you into that place with Holy God. Very likely you were going through some cataclysmic ordeal, and in the midst of it, you, in prayer, abandoned yourself to Christ as your only hope, with complete submission and surrender to Him. He became sufficient with His control in your life, (**Romans 12:2**), and you were overwhelmed by His Grace.

Each one of these encounters of brokenness and trials was and is a stair step to a deeper, more profound walk with God. As you experience this in your daily life, instead of being overcome by constant tribulations and filled with fear and anxiety, your daily life becomes and remains a phenomenal adventure of walking daily in the Spirit as He extends His Life through you. This same thing happened in Job when he saw God, and then he saw himself. In his desire to be one with God, Job violently assaulted the Kingdom of God, (*Matthew 11:12*). Because Job had learned of God in his youth, and had practiced the principles of what he heard and knew, he was wonderfully blessed of The Father. As he became broken and shattered, he was filled with the Glory of God's Presence. A proper foundation was finally laid, upon which God could build His Ministry. Look again at Job's words: "I must have you, Father. I love you. You are my sovereign. I totally abandon myself to you. Give yourself to me."

Like Job, each Christian will observe the results of brokenness. Where had Job been sitting for all of these chapters? In the ash pit of repentance, confessing his sins over and over to God. He was trying to repent in dust and ashes as he stated in *Job 7:20*, "*I have sinned; what shall I do unto thee, O thou preserver of men?*" In other words, "What else do you want, God? I have done my best to get your forgiveness." He repented, but God would not accept it. Somebody once told me that all I had to do was confess my sin and God would forgive me. How tragic this false doctrine! It does not release men into the forgiveness of God and into His Will! Many have taken *I John 1:9* as a license to steal. We must understand, however, that there is no true repentance until there is true brokenness by conviction. Only then will we see what God sees, confessing sin from a contrite heart. God forgives us and cleanses us from all unrighteousness solely from a broken heart. That's what happened to Job. He saw himself as God saw him. In the sixth verse of *Job 42*, he stated in brokenness, "*Wherefore I abhor myself, and repent in dust and ashes.*"

HE TOOK THE TEST

God met Job when he saw himself as he really was, and was broken over his life. God received his confession of true repentance and set him free; however, not completely. Many times in brokenness and restoration a testing occurs. Let's examine how God accomplished this in Job's life. As we see, he was filled with the Glorious Presence of God. The boils, however, remained. He was probably praising the Lord, weeping over his glorious relationship. First of all, there were tears of remorse of his own past sin, and then tears of rejoicing for God's forgiveness and presence in his life, (*Psalms 126:5*).

Almost immediately, however, God "squeezed the lemon" again to see what still remained. God spoke to Job's friends from the whirlwind and said to them in *verse 7*, *"Ye have not spoken of me the thing that is right, as my servant Job hath."* What was the "thing" to which God referred? I believe that God was speaking of Job's confession of sin as revealed to him by God through brokenness. So God, at the spiritual level of these men, dealt with them from the Old Testament's position, and that is the "shedding of blood for the remission of their sins." He told them to take seven bullocks and seven rams and *"go to my servant Job, and offer up for yourselves a burnt offering."* Upon completion of this step, God said, *"My servant Job shall pray for you; for him will I accept: lest I deal after your folly, in that ye have not spoken of me the thing which is right, like my servant Job."*

Now, again, let's not lose this perspective. I feel that it was more of a test in righteousness for Job than it was for these men. It was, however, imperative for them to be forgiven. For where "little is given, little is required; where much is given, much is required." God was preparing Job for his greatest ministry yet to come. In the meantime, Job had just committed all back to God. He had transferred ownership of his life (*Roman 12:1-2*). He had replaced his heart with the Heart of God, and desired with all passion, to hold tight upon the Father's Will and to walk in His Way.

I can see it now. Here they came, leading these animals over to Job, as he sat in the ashes. They stood there, with their heads hung in embarrassment, explaining to Job what God had said to them. I believe they desperately feared rejection by Job in their hearts. Having just experienced the Presence of God, having heard His Command, they probably stood terrified throughout the entire ordeal. One by one, these animals were slain in the presence of Job.

Now, the test. Upon completion of the sacrifice, they asked Job to pray for them as God had commanded. If any pride remained within the heart of Job, he would have looked at those men and said, "No. You accused me. You rejected me. You would not accept me and my righteousness and the activity of my life. You blamed me and I will not pray for you, for you deserve exactly what God is going to do to you. How dare you not stand with me. How dare you not pity me, oh ye, my friends."

But you see, my beloved, when a person has been touched by God and has permitted God to consume his life, his whole psychological quotient is changed by God's invading presence. The Bible says in *Matthew 5:3*, "*Blessed are the poor in spirit: for theirs is the Kingdom of Heaven.*" Job was so desperately in love with the Father and so exalted in his spirit by God's Glory, that he became overwhelmed with love for these who had come into his presence first to accuse him and then to beg for his prayers. When you love God to the point of self-abandonment, the unlovely become lovely as the Father consumes your life and loves through you, the evidence being an abounding love for those who dispitefully use you and persecute you. We find this obvious in God's Plan for His own Son, as the Bible declares, *"For God so loved the world, that He gave His only begotten Son..."*

Professor Stewart Blackie of Edinburgh University was lecturing one day when a student stood, holding the Bible in his left hand. The young man began reading a passage when the Professor roared at him, "Take your book in your right hand and be seated!"

The student never answered a word, but merely held up his right arm, which had been severed at the wrist. The Professor hesitated a moment, and with his face bathed in tears, went to the student and said, "I never knew about it. Will you forgive me?"

Years later, when this story was told at a Bible conference, a man with his right arm severed at the wrist arose and came forward saying, "I am the man that Professor Blackie led to Christ. But he never would have done it if he had not put his arms around me and made the wrong right!"

A beautiful verse that comes to mind at this point is *John 12:25*: *"He that loveth his life shall lose it; and he that hateth his life in this world shall keep it unto life eternal."* Job was already residing in the heavenlies. And, as the friends finished the sacrifice before God, Job prayed for them and God heard. It was the prayer of the Spirit of God through the mouth of His man. Though we'll never know its content, I can well imagine its power. What happened to those men was the beginning of eternal experiences in their lives.

But again, this was very likely a test for Job. Because of God's Glorious Presence, Job had completely renounced all bitterness in his heart. It was the burning out of the dross as he completely and totally submitted to God. He began, at that moment, to violently drive himself toward Him, as *Matthew 11:12* commands us to do. When he finished crying out to God for these friends, and all pride was dissolved in grace, the Lord moved upon Job's diseased body and completely healed him. *Verse 10* says, *"And the Lord turned the captivity of Job when he prayed for his friends."*

Now, what does that mean? Pride SATANICALLY captures the individual and keeps the demons in control, to feed upon the self-righteousness, anger, and hostility through unforgiveness, (*II Corinthians 2:10-11*). In Job's case, Satan placed a spirit of infirmity into his body when he touched him. God allowed this, (*I Samuel 16:14*). Job, however, still sore with pain, was filled with God and desired to pray for these men, (*Matthew 5:44*). At that moment, the wondrous Glory of God drove every spirit of infirmity out of his body! Job was healed. When a man puts God in the right place, which is first in his life, God's control in his life will be demonstrated before others. God will then be declared before men through the Person of Christ living through the freed person. It is a miraculous experience to be filled with the Holy Spirit!

Now, what were the final results of Job's transformation? The Scripture goes on to say that God gave Job twice as much as he had before. Into his life came children again -- seven sons and three daughters -- and Job lived one hundred forty years and saw his sons, and his sons' sons, even four generations. "When he died, he was old and full of days."

Now, why would God put that statement in this wonderful book? In *James 5:11*, the answer is given. *"Behold, we count them happy which endure."* In the Amplified Bible, this verse says:

> *"You know how we called those blessed (happy) who were steadfast -- who endured. You have heard of the endurance of Job; and you have seen the Lord's [purpose and how He richly blessed him in the] end, in as much as the Lord is full of pity and compassion and tenderness and mercy."*

My friend, the real story of Job's life and ministry is unwritten, and we will never know the final chapters until we get home. According to James, however, God required Job's brokenness so He could mightily use him in his last one-hundred forty years. If all scholarly accounts are right, he lived two hundred ten years. He was about seventy when his judgment began.

Oh, my beloved, to be used of God you must be contrite. If you desire to accelerate the procedure, to walk in what God is doing, then you must pray to be broken. Brokenness is a gift of Holy God. We must allow Him to break us of our flaws.

> *"The integrity of the upright shall guide them, but the willful contrariness and crookedness of the treacherous shall destroy them,"* (Proverbs 11:3).

Pray to be broken. It is a wonderful life.

CHAPTER THREE

SAME SONG, SECOND VERSE

"In the year that king Uzziah died I saw also the Lord sitting upon a throne, high and lifted up, and his train filled the temple. Above it stood the seraphims: each one had six wings; with twain he covered his face, and with twain he covered his feet, and with twain he did fly. And one cried unto another, and said, Holy, holy, holy is the Lord of hosts: the whole earth is full of his glory. And the posts of the door moved at the voice of him that cried, and the house was filled with smoke. Then said I, Woe is me! for I am undone; because I am a man of unclean lips, and I dwell in the midst of a people of unclean lips; for mine eyes have seen the King, the Lord of hosts. Then flew one of the seraphims unto me, having a live coal in his hand, which he had taken with the tongs from off the altar: And he laid it upon my mouth, and said, Lo, this hath touched thy lips; and thine iniquity is taken away, and thy sin purged. Also I heard the voice of the Lord, saying, Whom shall I send, and who will go for us? Then said I, Here am I; send me."
(Isaiah 6:1-8).

It must be understood that in every circumstance of tribulation in the Christian's life, he is to look for God's signature upon it as evidence of His involvement to get the attention of and to develop the life of an individual. The patterns of God's judgment, for the most part, are always the same. As we saw previously, Job began his youth by learning the truths of God and His Righteousness. As he began to conduct himself within that realm, the Old Testament laws involved expressed themselves into reality and blessing. As always, when one is newly born again, there is a complete thrust of his will toward God's Righteousness and Sovereignty. As a result, his walk with God is the strongest that it will be for a long period of time until, by the experience of brokenness his faith becomes even greater through the knowledge of God and His attributes, (*Hebrews 11:1*). At the beginning of this trust, when one is newly redeemed, faith is so childlike as one operates in the purity of belief. When one truly begins to focus on God's Word and His Life, the avenues toward His Will do not broaden, but become more narrow. In the final analysis, one does all things God's way, based on the truth of His Word and the level of this new believer's growth in faith.

God poured His blessings upon Job because he applied the Biblical principles that were given to him as a youth. Unable to handle it, there surfaced the true Job. He was then taken into chastisement and from there into scourging, and finally into the revelation of himself. In this process, he traveled through the door of repentance and into the pure vision of who God is. Better said, Job experienced brokenness. From that position, Job entered the transition of becoming less as God became more. Oh, how he loved God from that moment on!

This same kind of personal revelation was effectually given and transcribed in the life of another individual. Let's see the parallels of God's working. Such is the sixth chapter of the Book of Isaiah. For five chapters this remarkable prophet was an oracle of God, declaring the Truth of God. And yet he would be brought into a new dimension of revelation, far beyond anything that anyone had experienced as an Old Testament prophet.

No one will ever truly see Christ for who He really is, except through brokenness and tears. For brokenness to come, one's heart must be truly repentant, thereby crucifying the old man within him. Purging through real repentance and the revelation of personal sins must occur. Anger must be nailed to the cross. Lust, guilt, pride, and the rest of the flesh's control, must be put in its place. Complete abandonment to God must take precedence in the life of that individual.

When a person is completely broken over what he is, and ardent repentance overwhelms his sin, the Light of God's Spirit begins to shine inward to reveal the reality of His Righteousness and the purity of His Person. In that state, the believer is completely broken before God and ready for His Will and Ministry to be performed through his life. He must seek after it.

After much study I personally believe that Isaiah's experience was one of brokenness, to prepare him for the revelation of who God was/is, through the birth of His Son as He came through the womb of a virgin woman. He would come to this world in the flesh as God Incarnate, and would live a sinless life, that He might become sin for us. From there, He would be led as a sheep to the slaughter, silent before His accusers, to be nailed to a cross. He would then die a death so far beyond any human experience that even "His visage was marred more than any man." Physically, every bone would be poured out like water, meaning all would be out of joint, (Psalm 22:14). His blood would flow from His body as He would hang upon the cross. In the meantime, this event in history would cause even the sun to be blotted out and the earth to shake. Jesus would then be lain in the grave. Peace would falsely abound and the world's religious system would be brought to a calm again. Suddenly, that grave would open and a three-day dead body would come forth, risen alive from the grave! (We will show the real meaning of this in a later chapter.)

For someone to prophesy these events, however, would not only provide a vision for future notes of Biblical history of the Old Testament, but would also provide research for man, that they may declare a coming Messiah. It even extends beyond that, as is the difference of the sunrise to the sunset. It was in actuality, the beginning of a true new-world order in a new day that would have its birth on the morning of Pentecost, when the Holy Spirit would come. Such was the preparation of this announcement and its declaration. The pure truth of the matter in these verses of *Chapter 6* is that the man Isaiah is being made ready to share the greatest event of all human history: the coming Messiah, known as *"Wonderful, Counsellor, The mighty God, The everlasting Father, The Prince of Peace," (Isaiah 9:6), Jesus.*

What was about to happen in Isaiah's life was not just to get his attention, but to pierce to the deepest core of his innermost being, thereby bringing into union with his spirit the presence of the Holy Spirit of God. So it was when Isaiah raised his eyes in the Presence of God, and saw the Lord sitting on the throne, (*Isaiah 6:1-2*). "... *high and lifted up and his train filled the temple.*"   Then he saw above it the seraphims. "...*each one had six wings; with twain he covered his face, and with twain, he covered his feet and with twain he did fly.*" There are only a few Biblically-recorded experiences so clearly profound as that which happened to Isaiah that day. Truly, "*Our God is an awesome God; He reigns from heaven above.*"

Isaiah is being readied by God to receive the message of His coming Son and to have it burned deep into his heart. We find basically woven through every verse of this book, from that moment on, the wonderful presence of the Person of Jesus Christ, as well as the Holiness of God.

In the light of this, you will find that the usual procedure that God uses to bring an individual into true ministry is to first reveal Himself to him. Then in that encounter, he sees himself as God sees him. From there, he is shattered over his unrighteousness. Finally, he enters into a ministry that is no longer his, but God's. This is God's Biblical pattern, and over the years I have personally experienced it in my own life. Also, I have observed others through whom He extended His Will.

With this pattern in mind, let's see how God dealt with the prophet Isaiah. First of all, Isaiah saw himself after seeing God. By Scriptural example, God revealed everything about Himself to Isaiah: His throne, His heaven, and His presence as Light. Yet the Bible tells us that "no one has ever seen God and lived." But there are 44 recorded appearances of God in the Bible. The Hebrew word is "Ra-ah," which means, "to see clearly". Therefore, in whichever way God appeared to Isaiah, it forever changed the course of his life and ministry; for it began the disintegration of pride and flesh and birthed a man totally committed to God.

Remember, when Isaiah saw God, he saw himself. This must always happen to be used of God. Now, look back at his procedure of repentance. The first thing he said was, "Woe is me. I am undone." He, for the first time, saw himself as only God could see him. The level of unrighteousness was so overwhelming that he cried in agony before the Lord. He could not believe his own observation. We must understand that no one will ever be mightily used of God until all of self is unveiled and is purged by an inward desire to be broken.

At the moment God revealed Himself, Isaiah broke before His presence. Again, when a man truly sees in himself what God sees he will be exposed to what he really is in the eyes of God, even though he may feel he has done his best for God. He will, at that point, be shattered.

My beloved friend, there is no way you can serve God in the flesh. True ministry does not begin until He ministers through you. The tragedy of it all is that the churches are missing the two major doctrines regarding brokenness: One is the believer's total transformation into the image of God. The other missing doctrine is that the believer must be filled with the Spirit of God. I agree that many work hard at being religious and serving in activities in Christendom. But, in this end time of history, it has lost its place and power with God. In addition, if they are really dedicated, they labor to keep the law and structure of their particular denomination in order that they may prove that it is the only true doctrinally-pure group around. The immense problem with all of this, however, is that there are over 20,000 "Christian" denominations around the world. I'm not speaking of other groups who do not believe in God and Christ. I'm speaking of people who have taken their absolute truths from the Word of God, the Bible, and feel that they stand sovereignly in the center of the Will of God. They know their doctrine is the purest.

"An entry in the diary of Oswald Chambers reads like this: 'Mr. Swan was addressing some Christian Effendis and called me over to tell them what I considered the real danger of theological training. I promptly said, 'Swelled head,' and explained my belief that the only way to maintain spiritual life along with intellectual life was by the submission of the intellect to Jesus Christ, and that then intellect became a splendid handmaiden of the Lord; that intellect should be the feet and not the head of the student. I gave them Philippians 3:10'.

Edwin and Lillian Harvey

Satan has authored religions to keep men powerless and busy, rather than broken. This is I believe the *"spiritual wickedness in high places,"* spoken of in Ephesians. His object is to get men to focus upon promotion, rather than prayer. Thus, the church of today, for the most part, is dead. The world is dying, and no effort of religious busy-ness can stop it. Our salt is stepped on and our light is dim, if not out. There is no hope except a return to God on His terms. If however, the church did return, He would visit his people. He promised He would, (*II Chronicles 7:14*).

So, to be used of God we must first see what God sees in our lives. This is the reason for fasting. Denying food is not for the purpose of getting God involved in what we are doing, but to get us involved in God's Will, that we may be broken before the Lord. Fasting, in its right perspective, breaks the soul from submitting to the wiles of the flesh, and submits it instead to the Spirit of God within.

In Isaiah, we note again the classic move of God in the heart of a man, to bring him into His Will. As Job, Isaiah was required to see himself as God saw him. Only then would Isaiah be able to truly repent. Without revelation of who you are in the sight of God, the only thing you can do is rededicate your life to the efforts of activity in your religion. "Rededication" is a non-Biblical word used by many church denominations to give people an avenue back to structured activity, with little or no conviction of their sins.

The flesh cannot be rededicated except to religious performance, because rededication is non-Biblical. To be truly used of God, the believer must daily crucify the flesh. Crucifixion is applied when the believer energetically and dynamically drives his life back toward God. The Scripture profoundly states that as Christians we must daily return to God and His will. We are to "hunger, thirst, seek, knock, strain, pursue, chase, assault with violence", or "labor to enter into the rest." The Old and New Testaments are filled with ways that we are to "draw nigh." Incidentally, it is classic that when we enter into that rest, or are broken before God, we cease from our own works. Then and only then do we begin the activity of God, first to our hearts inwardly and then through our lives outwardly.

Romans 12:1-2 teaches us that Paul begged the Christians "to present their bodies a living (physically alive), sacrifice, (soulishly dead)", according to God's holiness. It is our "reasonable service". *Verse 2* describes the blessing of our obedience. We will no longer be conformed to the world, which incidentally, is the system of religion. In those days, Christians were circumcising their male children to prove their Christianity. He said, "It is not the circumcision of the flesh, but it is the cutting away of the 'old man'," (*Colossians 2:11*). In other words, "don't be conformed to the world or religious activities."

Then God declared that we are to be transformed. "Metamorphosis" is the word in the Greek, with the example of the caterpillar changing to a butterfly. In this case, the finished product of this encounter is the renewing of our mind. In one instance, our thinking is ground-bound to religious activity and dogma. Yet, when we become transformed, we become filled with His Mind, (spiritually-minded). That is, our minds and lives will no longer do things for God. Instead, His Mind will actively bring to pass His Will through our bodies. He will conduct His business through our beings because we have yielded ourselves totally to Him. The profound truth of the Word of God is truly *"Christ in you, the hope of glory,"* (*Colossians 1:27*).

You will never be transformed, filled, spiritually-minded, or usable until you are broken before God.

Psalm 51:17 shares:

"The sacrifices of God are a broken spirit: a broken and a contrite heart, O God, thou wilt not despise."

STOP THE WORLD, I WANT TO GET OFF

To understand what God was doing in preparing Isaiah for the revelation of Christ's life, let's review again what happens when a person is broken over what he is. First, he sees himself as God sees him. In that encounter he is devastated over the sin in his own life. No matter how righteous he appears to be to others, or even to himself, something profoundly happens to the person just as it happened to Job. Isaiah says of himself, *"I am a man of unclean lips."* He was undone when he saw himself through God. Similar circumstances challenged *Job in the 38th chapter*. When he saw God, he saw himself for the first time, and his declaration to God was that he was *"vile."*

Secondly, as in Job's sequence of breaking, Isaiah's revelation led him to confess of his own life, *"I am a man of unclean lips."* Now, don't miss the truth of this confession. He wailed, *"Woe is me. I'm undone."* In essence, *"Oh, God, I am vile.*" Job too declared this of himself as he saw himself through God. Isaiah then tells the "why" of his statement: *"Because I am a man of unclean lips..."* How much more could be written at this point! It must be understood that God teaches in His Word that, "it is not what goes into a person's mouth that defiles him; it is what comes out". Your confession broadcasts your real character and sets the course of your life, (*James 3:6*).

As I mentioned earlier, we conducted a study several years ago on the subject of negative confession. What started out to be a simple sermon turned into a major series, and finally a book that we originally entitled, "Death and Life are in the Power of the Tongue," Later, we changed the title to "God's Answer to the Critical Christian: K.Y.M.S.," or, "Keep Your Mouth Shut."

At this writing, I have been 36 years in the ministry. As I look back across the spiritual diary of my life, I cannot recall ever meeting an individual that God profoundly used that was critical or negative. It seems, however, that every one of those that walked in victory had a realm of brokenness, displayed by a supernatural prayer level. When they saw a person taken in a fault, rather than being critical of him or putting him down verbally, they were broken over his circumstances and prayed for him. It is an extreme evidence of maturity when a Christian is able to control his lips, (*James 3:2*). It is at that point that "he can control his whole body" and "present himself as a living sacrifice to God".

In regard to this, and with him now in the presence of God, we find that Isaiah cried out, *"I am a man of unclean lips."* He, however, took it a step further. He said, *"I dwell in the midst of people of unclean lips."* Now, examining this statement discloses that not only did Isaiah very likely speak negative words, but he listened to the negative words of others. A great barometer of your spiritual walk with God would be to admit how you feel when people around you become critical of others. Mark it down. If you join in or listen without being grieved in your spirit, you are completely and absolutely separated from the Holy Spirit's control. It will be evidenced by an absence of answered Prayer. Again, the only sign of spiritual maturity is God's extension of His Life through you. Your Prayers will be answered because His will shall be accomplished through you.

It is interesting to note God's position on negative words as taught in *Proverbs 6:12*. The Bible declares, "*A naughty person, a wicked man, walketh with a froward mouth.*" Such was Isaiah's proclamation. He was a man of unclean lips. Now, the word "naughty" in that *12th verse* is the Hebrew word "beliyaal," which literally means, "a man of flesh or evil." The Greek word for belial is "satan." After Isaiah was crushed by God's revelation to him, he was able to recognize of himself, "*My speaking is unclean.*" It is controlled by Satan.

Then, in the light of Isaiah's further revelation of himself, he says, "*I dwell in the midst of a people of unclean lips.*" In his brokenness before God, his sins became manifest in his heart. We will always see our true selves when we see God through our tears, whether they be tears of remorse or of rejoicing. For Isaiah's statement, in essence, is that "*I not only speak gossip, but I listen also.*" God says in *Proverbs 17:4*, "*A wicked doer giveth heed to false lips and a liar giveth ear to a naughty tongue.*" Not only does Satan seek to control our speaking, but also our listening, thereby destroying our walk in the Spirit of God. Gossip is best defined by the statement, "If you are not a part of the problem or the solution, but are involved then you are a part of gossip, which is Satan's tool to divide and destroy."

I must repeat that in close to 3,000 meetings and speaking engagements, I have never met a spiritually mature individual, (evidenced by answered prayer) that exhibited a critical or negative personality. Satan operates in death. Jesus operates in life, (*Proverbs 18:21*). When people are alive in Jesus Christ by the Power of His Glory in and through their lives, they "*refrain his tongue from evil and his lips that they speak no guile.*"

When Isaiah came face-to-face with God in his spirit, the encounter, again, was for one purpose, and that was to burn out of him all that was "self" or flesh. In so doing, God then within Isaiah's knowledge, through the Spirit, prophesied the coming of His Son. To begin, God purged his lips. Then, He purged his hearing. He literally transformed his life to establish the mind of God within him, (*Romans 12:1-2*). Does all of this sound familiar? When Job came face-to-face with God, he saw himself. He cried, as Isaiah, "*I am vile.*" He then stated that he would "*lay his hand upon his mouth.*" His final declaration to God was, "*I will proceed no further.*" Basically, he was saying, "Stop the world, I want to get off." "I am through with knowing about You (religion). I want to know You, God." Pride personified states, "I will." As Lucifer declared his authority in heaven through the five "I wills," so does Satan in his fallen state continue to work through man's spirit by pride. When the devil consumes the life of an individual, he continues his work through that person. The tragedy is that it works in religion. In fact, for the most part, pride is what makes religion work.

Beloved, when you're broken, you will cease from your works. Birthed in you will be an explosion of God's Spirit, and through you shall be the ministry of His Will. Then to you will come His life of joy unspeakable! It is life beyond description, "peace that passes all understanding," "love, joy, peace," all of the attributes of *Galatians 5:22-24*. Only when the Spirit has consumed your life do you walk in Christ. Oh, wondrous joy! Oh, marvelous grace! Victory in Jesus!

As David Wright stated in his short poem,

"Looking upward full of grace
He prayed, and from a happy place,
God's glory smote him in the face."

The Scripture says in **Psalms 34:5**, **"They looked to Him, and were radiant"** (**Amplified**). Oh, the joy of the transformed life!

As we read in Job, he saw himself when he saw God, and was broken over what he witnessed. He confessed the iniquity of his mouth. Then, as we read in **Job 40:5**, Job makes a startling statement which, in sequence, happened to Isaiah: "**I will proceed no further.**"

From this parallel, we look at Isaiah. Here we find the same scenario. His confession was purged and his position changed. **Proverbs 18:21** states it well:

"Death and life are in the power of the tongue
and they who indulge it shall eat the fruit of it
[for death or life]." **Amplified**

Now, many have taken the first part of that verse and used it colloquially, or referred to it in teaching or preaching, missing the true meaning of the entire verse.

Someone well said, "You are what you say." For instance, if you awaken depressed and you declare, "It's going to be one of those days," then you have set in your life the course or direction of what you will experience. Satan takes your words and moves them against you or against others as you speak negative confession.

It is so simple to discern the spiritual status of a church in which we minister. When we walk into the building, if the atmosphere is oppressed and bound, it is usually from the critical or negative talk of its members. This creates a vast hindrance to the Word and its message, not only to the preaching, but also to the hearing from God. This encumbrance is evidenced by a division within the body that comes from negative, critical confession. The atmosphere is demonically filled due to the absence of the Spirit of God and Prayer. Sweet and bitter water will not come from the same well, (*James 3:10-11*).

In fact, *James 3:6* asserts:

"So is the tongue among our members, that it defileth the whole body and setteth on fire the course of nature."

How powerful are your words! Such is the meaning of *Proverb 18:21*: *"If you speak death, you live death. If you speak life, you live life"*. It also goes on to say in that verse that *"those who love to speak death shall eat the fruit thereof"*. By the same token, those who speak life shall have life and will walk within that realm of victory. You are what you say, and you live what comes out of your mouth.

It is imperative that you control your lips. Satan knows what to do to destroy you. He will set you up in "wiles" or situations just to get you to be critical of yourself or others. He can at that point order and set the course of your life. Your trip to God's Will through brokenness is immediately stopped and you lose ground, (*Matthew 15:11*).

James 3:2 reaffirms: *"For in many things we offend all. If any man offend not in word, the same is a perfect man, and able also to bridle the whole body."*

In the light of this, I have never seen the truth of this passage to fail. Those who can hold their confession, their critical words, and their negative speaking, are able to present their bodies as a living sacrifice back to God. Satan knows, however, that he can set up circumstances to create a diversion within a carnal Christian. This person is focused on himself, and does not set his eyes upon God in praise. He is openly negative and Satan "comes in like a flood," (*I Corinthians 3:1-6*).

So much more is said about this in *Ephesians 4*, *James 3*, and *I Peter 3*. *Ecclesiastes 5* is classic in its study of confession! Hundreds of verses have been placed throughout the Word of God to convict us to keep our minds and lives under the control of God's Spirit. We eat the fruit of our confession. The first lesson we learn in brokenness is not to speak until spoken through.

So, God was preparing Isaiah for the most phenomenal experience any prophet would ever have. He would see by the revelation of the Holy Spirit, the birth of Jesus, His life, His death, and resurrection. God would also reveal to Isaiah the birthing of the Spirit into the hearts of men, bringing victory into their lives, and changing them into the image of Christ. To receive this revelation, Isaiah had to be broken. Again, Isaiah was undone because he was "a man of unclean lips," and "I dwell in the midst of a people of unclean lips." How did he know this? What made him aware of it? The fifth verse of *Isaiah 6* tells us: "*for mine eyes have seen the King, the Lord of Hosts.*" Does all of this sound familiar to you? God used this same procedure in Job's life to prepare him for His Will. God takes the same course today when filling an individual with His Spirit. He must be filled to be used. The book of Isaiah so resembles the message of Job that it is "the same song, second verse".

My beloved, to be used of God, you must be conquered. For this to happen, you must see God in your spirit man. Upon seeing Him and standing in the Light of His Presence, you will be exposed to the darkness of your true self. Having observed Him as He is, you will crumble with conviction as your life passes through your mind. The revealing of yourself will induce in you a cry for Him, "Oh God, oh God, forgive me." True repentance will not manifest until the Spirit of God reveals to you the "who and what" you really are, (*Psalm 51:17*). Then, in that transformed state, there will no longer be any embarrassment, for you will then openly confess your sins, (*James 5:16*), and be cleansed in the experience. Consider again Job's cry in *Chapter 42* as the Spirit of God was revealed to him: "I beseech thee," or, "I demand of thee," was Job's request. "*Declare thou unto me*," in that "I must have you God, totally and completely. I want you to be the Lord of my life."

From the position of absolute abandonment to God with his soul, God moved in and declared Himself to Job. From that moment on, it became paramount to Job to know and walk with God. This encounter with God, through brokenness, will cause you to desire to become God's total property, ready for the design of His Will as it consumes your nature. Suddenly, unlovely people will become lovely to you. The things that you feared He would do if you submitted to Him will also be made lovely and acceptable to you. You will be overwhelmed by the urge to do them as you cry, "Oh, God, any time, any place, any where. I must have you. Please give Yourself to me." Both Job and Isaiah beheld the Presence of God. Isaiah's response was, "*For mine eyes have seen the King, the Lord of Hosts.*"

Now, in continued preparation of Isaiah for God's ministry, there was yet a work to be done to his lips. God, in order to use this man, was to do a final purging of his confession, that he might, as I said earlier, come to a place where he would not speak until spoken through. God then sent one of the seraphims to Isaiah, "having a live coal in his hand which he had taken with the tongs from off the altar." Now, did he place it upon his head that he might have brilliancy of mind to speak the truth? No. Did he lay it upon Isaiah's feet that he might have direction of service and the opportunity to declare the message? Absolutely not. He laid it upon the lips of Isaiah that God might purge from the prophet all indication of self, desire, negative confession, and critical words. He literally burned (cauterized) his lips to such a degree that not only were they spiritually seared, destroying all negativity, but they were sealed for a lifetime of service as an oracle of God.

Fire is the greatest agent of purity that exists. Nothing that is living can stand its attack. When that live coal from the altar of God touched the lips of Isaiah, the anointed testimony of the truth of holiness and the power of God was attained. Incidentally, as you read the rest of **verse 7**, you will find that when God purged Isaiah's lips, He also took away his iniquity and cleansed his sins. This is the true evidence of brokenness. Again, if people would understand the amount of bondage brought about in their lives because of their confession, they would comprehend the truth of keeping their mouths shut. A negative tongue is rebellion to God. In the light of this, the Bible states that "**rebellion is as the sin of witchcraft,**" and witchcraft is the Hebrew word for "whispering." Being negative and critical is a sign of being under demonic control. Satan does his work by words.

Now, in review of the events leading to his brokenness, we find that Isaiah saw the Lord. He then saw himself and was devastated and cried in true repentance for forgiveness. In progression, God then purged his confession and changed the course, or direction, of what proceeded out of Isaiah's mouth.

When we see God and are broken, and our confession is cleansed, suddenly our ears are clear to hear the voice of God's Will. Spiritual ears were placed within Job and Isaiah during the process of their breakings. From the presence of the temple, God suddenly cried out, *"Whom shall I send and who will go for us?'"* Isaiah heard the cry and responded. It is amazing how tribulation will tune the believer's hearing to God's frequency.

Each day of the Christian's life has already been written out. The Bible, in *Ephesians 2:10*, proclaims that God has laid out *"paths which He prepared ahead of time*." (*Amplified*) We are to get up each morning and transfer our bodies to Him by praying, "Father, in the name of Jesus Christ, I give you my life today." We remain in praise until we have the peace of God consuming our hearts, and the knowledge that He has heard us and answered.

We then move from that position into the activities of our day. We have yielded to His Will, or that which is of His Kingdom, that we might experience what is to be **"done on earth as it is in heaven."** The true Will of God is practicing the Presence of Christ. God can then speak to us intuitively and direct our steps. He becomes our light and lamp, and through us ministers His Will. We, in our Christian adventure, begin to *"walk in the light*." *"Works which He prepared ahead of time,"* or His ministry through us is perfected. As Jesus was an extension of the Father here upon this earth, so we are an extension of the Son. Only the broken individual is able to hear in his spirit, and walk in what he hears. He shall operate according to that procedure.

Isaiah had been broken. He had confessed his major sin. Suddenly, his hearing was opened as God said, *"Whom shall I send and who will go for us?'"* With the quickest response came this man Isaiah, declaring back to God, "**Here am I; send me**." In essence, "I beg you to take my life. I must have you God."

Now this, again, was as the test of Job. As you recall, upon being broken, Job begged God for His relationship, that they might be one together. Job repented because of brokenness. He loved God beyond anything he had ever known. God tested his walk by sending the friends to him, that he might sacrifice for them. It was a trial, I believe, to see if the bitterness was gone because his friends had bailed out and had begun to accuse him. Yet his love for God was so overwhelming and so beyond anything that he had ever known. He could not have cared less what his flesh had experienced in sickness, anger, and hostility. They were not even worthy to be compared to the glory being revealed to him now! He cried out to God for relationship. Then, when he sacrificed for his friends, God healed him.

Oh, blessed, precious Father, how many times you have put us in the midst of great conflict only to bring us to a oneness with you. In that desperation, when all of the doors were closed and there was no hope, the moments of tears and complete yielding to you brought peace in the midst of the prayer. Because of that peace, we could declare our prayers as answered, without knowledge of how You would complete them. Oh, wonderful Father! Blessed Jehovah! Precious Jesus Christ who dwells within! How much you would do for us if we would allow it! And how much you would do through us if we were broken over what we are, (*Isaiah 66:2*)!

There is a quote that applies here. The author is unknown. "God has two thrones, the one in the highest heavens, the other in the lowest hearts."

Beloved, I beg you to experience what it's like to walk in Him. As I have asked time and again in this chapter, and in others, "would you abandon yourself to God?" So few have. Those that do will make great the turning points in history. Only then will nations change directions, causing people to be swept into the Kingdom of God through the effort of prayer that is empowered by the Glorious Presence and Will of God. Read the Book of Isaiah and see how the language of his prophecies changed from that moment of encounter with God. See a heart so yielded to God that our Father was able to declare through him the majesty of His Son. Isaiah, by inspiration, called Him *"Wonderful, Counsellor, the mighty God, The everlasting Father, The Prince of Peace."* Oh, the privilege that Isaiah beheld, seeing Him with eyes from which scales had fallen. No longer would the law dictate the direction of His efforts. Grace instead would enter into the heart of this man and begin to fashion through prophecy the Kingdom of God Incarnate, and His Righteousness.

Don't miss the experience. It's not an option. We are commanded to be filled with the Spirit, (*Ephesians 5:18*). It is the resurrected life. Please understand, it is not a present to be given to you by someone; it is the person of Christ who has been given through you to the lives of others. Let Him who is within consume that which is without. Pray to be broken. Beg God. Get out of the business of the Christian life and into the fullness of Christ, for Christ truly is our life. Be broken. Ask for it. Beg for it. Fast for it. It is wonderful!

CHAPTER FOUR

JESUS PAID IT ALL

When something is of God, it must have a Biblical precedent. Such is the case for brokenness in the Bible. Through cause and effect we go further into the Book of Isaiah and experience with him the revelation of the coming Messiah and His Miraculous Life. Once more, it is my belief that Isaiah was broken by God so that he could reveal to man the wondrous life of Christ through his book. To understand the reason for brokenness we must realize, based on the Word of God, that all true ministry that we have is what Christ does through us. All the rest, as I have stated earlier, is Christians doing Christian activity based on the concepts of man. Another word for it is religion. And again, in this present day, we have thousands of different groups or denominations from which to choose. Remember also, that God has maintained His True Church even through all the confusion of religion over the years. In essence, then, pure ministry is not from what a believer knows to do based on what he has been taught, but what is done through him after the experiences of a broken heart and prayer. Such was the position of Christ here upon this earth as He prepared Himself for our redemption and eternal salvation. And we, beloved, cannot begin in our finite minds to fathom the price that was paid for it.

No faithful ministry that is real will ever be performed except from a righteousness position. Again, that word means "right standing with God," or better said, "standing right where God is." This comes only from our putting ourselves in that place by such desire and desperation that we labor our way to a state of being filled and operating in His Glory, (*Hebrew 4:11*).

Make no mistake, the true Christian life is a battle. It begins in a "trial" with our own flesh, (*James 1:2-4 Amplified*), that it might be broken and submitted to control by God's Spirit. This contention becomes a denial of our own righteousness. The old sin nature seeks the desire and designs of men, opposing God's nature and the control of the Holy Spirit. We must be broken, as Jesus Christ experienced brokenness in His own life in order that He might be all that God would have Him be here upon this earth, in payment for our sins.

JESUS NEVER WORKED A MIRACLE

In this chapter, we're going to deal with the road that our Lord traveled, and the patterns set by Him for our example. Remember, all of Christ's ministry was the life of the Father through Him. He did not make the blind to see, the lame to walk, or the maimed's hands to be made whole. He performed no miracles here upon this earth. All the wonders that were done were in answer to prayer, for Jesus came as the Son of man, though He was the very Son of God. Even as He was opened, broken, and spilled out, so we must be also if He shall live through our lives. Jesus said of Himself that He could do nothing. God's Power through Him performed the word.

In *John 5:17, 19, and 30*, Jesus declares of Himself, "*I can of mine own self do nothing.*" All of the profound occurrences as Jesus walked upon this earth, were the manifestations of the Glory and Power of God through the Son, in answer to the prayers of Jesus. Christ constantly "went apart to pray." Oh beloved, Grace through prayer, extends from us into the lives of others the Miracle of God's Power and His Glory. We, however, must be broken as was Jesus. To be able to hear someday as we stand before him, "*Well done, thou good and faithful servant,*" is the greatest reward of heaven.

To have that happen, we must be as contrite as Jesus when He wept before the Father in agonizing prayer. The Word gives an account of His brokenness in *Hebrews 5:7-9*. Not only did He pray specific prayers from the mind of the Father, but "*His supplications were with strong crying and tears*." Jesus constantly wept for us while praying before God.

In the Amplified, this verse reads, "*He was heard because of His reverence toward God*." Beloved, please understand that the word "reverence" means to be "submitted," "dedicated," "yielded," "worshipful," and totally given over to God, and that in desperation you beg to be used of Him. Then, as we've said time and again, to be useful for God, we must abandon ourselves to Him, knowing that we have no righteousness within ourselves, for it is all as "filthy rags". From that position in our transformed righteousness, it suddenly becomes His life, for we're only as righteous as He is righteous in us. The level of brokenness in our lives is determined by our yieldedness to Him and to His consuming control over all that we are. In the case of the Scripture we just read, the words "*His reverence* "simply mean "Godly fear and piety." Jesus abstained from anything that would bring separation between the Father and Him. So must we be in Him.

Now, the Spirit was with Him. Incidentally, it is the same Spirit which indwells those of us who are born again. Many times, however, we discover that as we're about to enter into an event we become desperately uneasy inside, knowing that something is wrong. That uneasiness is the Holy Spirit speaking to your spirit in an effort to give you direction in a matter. The Scripture says that the Holy Spirit will guide us into all truth, (*John 16:13*). Jesus was so pure in His walk in the Spirit that He was never hindered by evil. He faced the sins that we face and stood totally against them. Such was His position with God, and so pure was His Heart toward the Father. The Amplified says, *"He shrank from the horrors of separation from the bright presence of the Father."*

Then, **Hebrews 5:8** says it all. *"Although He was a son, He learned [active, special] obedience through what He suffered,"* (**Amplified**). He left heaven. He came to earth virgin-born. He lived a life without sin, died on the cross, and rose from the grave. He destroyed all the power of the enemy through those events. He was God in the flesh. But it must be understood, Jesus was the Son of God as well as the Son of Man. As a human, He learned suffering. So must we learn obedience through suffering

Oh, my beloved, do not run from your tribulation. Submit sovereignly to God in praise in the midst of your trials. Become joyfully excited as you transfer your spirit to His allowing Him to consume you by taking those burdens from you as you *"cast all your care upon Him,"* (**I Peter 5:7**). So walk through your sorrows in righteousness, excitement, and joy, with *"peace of God that passeth understanding,"* (**Philippians 4:7**). Then you bear testimony to those around you of the sovereignty of a Holy God and His Presence in your life. Oh, for the privilege of being His! It can happen to all born-again believers who will fight their flesh and force themselves constantly toward Christ with all their hearts, (**Romans 12:1-2**).

Pray to be broken. **Hebrews 5:9** states of Jesus:

"His completed experience made Him perfect [in equipment]. He became the Author and Source of eternal salvation to all those who give heed and obey Him." (Amplified)

Now, that may not mean much to you at this point, but, my beloved, someday when you get home, having passed through this flesh either by death or by rapture, and you stand in the midst of God's Presence, you will be overwhelmed by the knowledge in your spirit in its glorified state of what Christ has performed for you. You will then fall at His feet crying, "Glory, worthy, worthy is the Lamb." You will praise Him! You will exalt Him! You will glorify His Name! It will be the spontaneous breaking of a wellspring within you. Oh, the joy you will experience at that point of sudden pure knowledge of who He is and what He has done. It is so far beyond all that you can conceive that it takes the sublimed mind to understand. You will then realize that He learned His obedience through what He suffered, and you will praise Him in pure adoration. What a price He paid for us!

Now, before we can move from this glorious truth of the breaking of Christ for His Ministry, we must realize that we are in co-identification with Him when we are broken, for only through this experience does He minister by way of His Life. In the book of *Isaiah*, we are given the message of how God prepared Christ for His Purpose and our redemption.

In *Chapter 53*, we have the Will of God through the mind of the prophet to give to us the description of what really happened to our Christ. *Verse 2* begins by telling us about Jesus' early years. *"As a tender plant and a root out of dry ground did He grow up."* The Bible then says that there was *"no beauty in Him,"* describing His physical features. God gave us a physical description of His Son. Jesus was a normal, every day, run of the mill, Jewish man. He was not strong, masculine, tall, commanding of appearance, or of great authority. He had not even a powerful voice that would startle a listener and claim his attention. God gave Him no beauty that any one would desire His Flesh or His Personality. You see, the ministry of Christ was to allow the Father to perform through Him so that by the work of the Father in Him, the world would know that Jesus was the Messiah.

How many times, through brokenness, have Christians discovered that the gifts or talents they were serving God with are of "none effect" and that it was their own choice for service but not His. I studied music and sang for a number of years in our meetings until eventually God took that completely away. Now, for others, singing may be a valid ministry, but for me it was not. People enjoyed our music and spoke highly of it, and yet in my spirit, I knew that many times I would sing to please the listener (and to sell my albums) rather than to minister God's Grace. There have also been lonely hours of standing in the pulpit without God's presence or covering, as I would try to preach without prayer or brokenness. The message had worked in other meetings, and for other men. So, I preached their work with great hope of having their same results.

I shared with someone recently that I have long since made a deal with God. I could preach or He could preach. If it was all right with Him, I would rather listen to Him than to me. Some of the most profound things that have ever come out of my mouth have come from beyond that which I had studied and far beyond my own personal mental ability. Those words had come only from the "well" of the Holy Spirit within. I have a tendency to preach angrily. When I'm not contrite in spirit, I can take the Truth of the Word of God and pound it upon the heads of people. The events in the course of my preaching have been tragic when I have allowed this! Yet, I can take the same truths, and in desperation before God, beg Him to speak through me and to break me. Then His glory is brought into the service. The results are so profound that only God can be honored. I know more than anyone that I have nothing to do with the outcome. How wonderful are these times with the Lord and it continues to be my earnest prayer that whatever it takes to break my life that He would do it. Ministry is so futile without Him, because it is not ministry, but manipulation.

R. A. Torrey said of Dwight L. Moody, "I think he was the humblest man I have ever known in all my life. He loved to quote the words of another: 'Faith gets the most; love works the most; but humility keeps the most.'"

Oh, how wondrous the joy and the peace of walking in His Will! But, my beloved friend, it comes not without tears. Tears of brokenness over what I am and then tears of joy over who He is. The result of that relationship is the awesome, glorious, wondrous experience of having ministered His Will. There are no words to express it. How great our God!

Let's look now at Christ's brokenness and His resulting ministry. From a position of obedience, Jesus came to this earth to fulfill one purpose: to die, to bear our sins in His Body on the tree. Not only did He bear our sins, He became sin for us. Jesus' human body was capable of anger, lust, greed, pride, and fear, as well as every human emotion. All of these things consume our flesh and are amplified by Satan's demonic spirits. They begin to overcome us if we lose control by non-praying. Remember, flesh out of control is spirit and there are only two kinds of spirits -- the Holy Spirit and the unholy spirit. Jesus experienced the same things that we encounter, and by violence, rejected them in driving Himself to the Father in constant prayer. In facing the *"like passions"* that we face, and by rejection of them, He made for us a way of escape through Him, (*Hebrews 4:15*). And yet, as in Christ's life, that way must be fought for, (*Matthew 11:12*). The flesh must be consumed. It must be crucified. A dead man will not struggle with his attacker, for his flesh ceases to be. Any movement would be caused by another source or force. Such is the resurrected life, as we yield our lives fully to Christ, (*Galatians 2:20*).

Now, let's examine the price that was paid for us that we might walk in its Glory. *Isaiah 53:3* says, "*He is despised and rejected of men.*" In this end time, there is a desperate move to marry religion with the world system as our denominations study how to meet people where they are and then try to compromise with them. Someone recently wrote a book entitled, Whatever Happened To Sin? That's a formidable question in this day as a truce with worldliness has taken the place of conviction. Confusion therefore, has entered the Christian experience. Instead, Christ should be the Sovereign over the Christian life. But, even in the typical Christian walk, there are no longer any absolutes. The end results historically are always judgment upon the land, (*Psalm 9:17*).

Where are the warriors? Where are the anointed men of the Bible who stood without fear before all? Even in the loss of their lives, how excited they were that the Holy Spirit had consumed them! Jesus' Total Self and ministry was extended through their persons and through their beings. They were filled with the Sovereignty and Presence of the Son of God. They constantly stood in awe as to what He was doing through them. Truly death had no sting, (*I Corinthians 15:55-56*).

How can we ever forget the words of Paul, who was not only old and physically cold, but spiritually bold as in the dungeon he cried out, "*That I may know Him and the power of His resurrection and the fellowship of His sufferings,*" (*Philippians 3:10*). My beloved, the same grace available two thousand years ago is also available today. Paul was dedicated, striving toward Jesus in joyous abandonment of his own life to Him. He constantly labored "*to enter into rest.*" In light of this, where are the warriors of today? Who can stand faced with despair and be transformed by praise? Who, devoid of pride, cares not whether they are received by those people who are about them? For God says of His own Son, "*He was despised and rejected of men. He was a man of sorrows. He was acquainted with grief. We hid, as it were, our faces from Him. He was despised and we esteemed him not."*

There are no words that can truly share with you the depth of these verses and what Christ felt from His human side. Please recall that He had a human body and was subject to "like passions" as we are. Yet, He constantly drove Himself to the Father in transforming prayer. He even counted the cross a joy. Yet we know he was a man of sorrows because He carried our sorrows. He carried our griefs in His body on the tree. They have been borne already. They are paid for. *"Rejoice and be glad," (Matthew 5:12, I Peter 4:13).*

Now, the Hebrew word for "sorrow" is "Choliy," which simply means "maladies." Not only did Jesus go to the cross for us, but He bore within Himself the feelings that we have: the hurts, the worries, the burdens. Again, when we stand before Him someday, we will have a pure understanding of all that He did. Yet, we will wonder why we did not yield more to him, permitting Him to consume us with His life, and that in all that was conflict in our lives, we could have stood in Him in great peace. Beloved, even in the face of His attackers and accusers, He experienced love for them. We can do the same in every event of tribulation, if we allow, through the Holy Spirit, His life to fill and overwhelm us.

You say, how can it be? Through the transformed life. How many times did He weep over those that were about him? Look as He surveys Jerusalem. His contrite, broken heart cries, *"If you would have only received me."* How many times did He look at the multitudes and become moved with brokenness and compassion? Even aware of the coming separation from God as He would hang upon the Cross, He cried to His Father from the garden, *"If thou be willing, remove this cup from me;*

nevertheless not my will, but thine, be done." You will find woven, all through the pattern of the four Gospels, the constant strand of tears as He was broken for those around Him.

The Cross was the reason for His coming. It is the culmination of all that involves eternity. For in hanging on the tree, "*He bore our griefs and carried our sorrows*." Yet, "we did esteem Him stricken, smitten of God and afflicted." For what reason? *Isaiah 53:5* says, "*He was wounded for our transgressions*," ours, yours, and mine; sins that we have committed. Placed upon Him were all the horrors of our lives, even those done in secret, whether they were mental sins or physically overt. It was our iniquities that bruised Him, for God says, "*The chastisement of our peace was upon Him and, with His stripes, we are healed.*"

As the song says ...

> "When I survey the wondrous Cross,
> On which the Prince of Glory died,
> My richest gain I count but loss
> And pour contempt on all my pride.
>
> Forbid it Lord, that I should boast,
> Save in the death of Christ, my God,
> All the vain things that charm me
> most,
> I sacrifice them to His Blood".
>
> Isaac Watts

Can you imagine the clamor that will sound when we enter into His Presence through death or rapture? Instantly, from this body to pure eternal Spirit, with glorified mind we will see what He has done for us. How we shall praise Him, and praise Him, and praise Him! Thank you, God. Thank you for Jesus. For we were "*sheep that had gone astray, each one his own way, but the Lord has laid upon Him the iniquity of us all,*" (*Isaiah 53:6*).

Now, remember that in order to experience Christ's life through us, we must enter into the same realm in which He walked to bring forth His Ministry. For it is through brokenness that we are birthed into the dimension of the victorious Christian life. To live from "glory to glory," we must go from breaking to breaking. At the end of each experience of brokenness is a new measure of the quality of Christ through our lives, and a deeper level of faith in which to believe Him. Awaiting, on the other side of tribulation is the ministry that has been written out for us in heaven, according to *Ephesians 2:10*. That ministry becomes, "*Thy kingdom come, thy will be done, on earth as it is in heaven.*" We focus our entire attention and life upon Christ. Through us, He begins to develop the character of His Will. From there, we move into a higher dimension of yieldedness to Him, growing in the attributes of His Life, which are "love, joy, peace," and all the rest of *Galatians 5:22-24*.

Paul knew this readily. He so enjoyed tribulation because Christ became more real and sufficient in every experience. Through each situation brokenness, he moved to a deeper level in his relationship with Christ. Again, find him in *Philippians 3:10* saying:

> "*... that I may know Him and the power of His resurrection and the fellowship of His sufferings, being made conformable unto His death.*"

Now, in the Amplified translation, Paul states that he wants to:

"... become more deeply acquainted with Him, perceiving and recognizing and understanding [the wonders of His person] more strongly and more clearly. And that I may, in the same way, come to know the power outflowing from His resurrection [which it exerts over believers]; and that I may so share His sufferings as to be continually transformed in spirit, into the likeness even, to His death [in the hope]."

Joyous, blessed brokenness! It is the bridge to righteousness and true ministry.

Philippians 3:10 so profoundly states here that the road which leads to the Will of God and His purpose in the heart of man is very rocky. In the midst of any conflict, however, the grace of God is joyously sufficient, even in overwhelming circumstances, if you will stay hand in hand with God Through Prayer. He will lead you through by His Spirit, (*Romans 8:14*). As this begins to happen more and more in your life, you will begin to look at your troubles through the eyes of God. From that position, you will truly understand the declaration that "all things work together for good, for those who love God with all of their hearts and are called into greater maturity according to His purpose as is every Christian," (my translation).

You see, if you are born again you were given a gift, a calling, and a ministry, (*Romans 12*) at the moment of your new birth. These came the instant the Holy Spirit took residence in your spirit. You must labor daily to enter into His Will. So, in the midst of the troubles that come, you drive yourself to Him in prayer. From there, He intervenes and overcomes by His Will, and you experience the wonderful presence and control of the Holy Spirit. Tribulation is truly for your good and His Glory (*Genesis 50:20*). Persecution is literally the purging of the soul and flesh, (carnality), in order to get you to abandon yourself to God through prayer, (*II Timothy 3:12*). Always remember that your response to tribulation reflects the level of your walk with God. *Philippians 3:11*, gives you the reason why Paul became so excited when tribulation came. He said, in the Amplified, "... *if possible that I may attain to the [spiritual and moral resurrection that lifts me] out from among the dead [even while in the body]*." God brings you out of dead, mortal, religious flesh through brokenness, that you "*might have life and have it more abundantly*," (*John 10:10*).

You say, "Brother Bonner, am I to go out and look for trouble?" No. You go out looking for Jesus. Abandon your life to our precious Lord with all of your heart. Begin to yield yourself to Him. Begin to pray that He will break you. Then hold onto Him in high praise regardless of any conflict. Incidentally, breaking will become a wonderfully common procedure in your life as you grow in the Lord. When grace becomes sufficient in your situations a new level of breaking will begin. As someone once said, "From that maturing point, you will begin to simply state when troubles comes, 'I wonder what God's up to in my life now.'" Always remember, as it is well noted in the Word, that God promised, "*My grace is sufficient for thee*," (*II Corinthians 12:9*). Always! Paul also stated in that verse, "*For my strength is made perfect in weakness. Most gladly therefore will I rather glory in my infirmities, that the Power of Christ may rest upon me*."

Edwin Harvey writes: "In an old magazine, the *Moody Church News*, a certain incident was related in which the narrator was conversing with a dear Christian brother. This friend was being greatly used of God to spread the Gospel through the printed page. In telling of how this great ministry came to him when he was without any visible resources, he uttered a profound statement well worth remembering: 'I learned,' said he, 'that there was one thing I could give to God that would add to His Perfection.'

'And what might that be?' inquired his friend. 'I have never thought of anything that one could give to God that would be an addition, in any sense or form.'

'Why,' was the reply, 'it is my weakness. His strength is made perfect in weakness.'"

Well, you say, "What do you want me to do?" Exactly what it says in that *fourteenth verse of Philippians 3*. "*I press toward the mark for the prize of the high calling of God in Christ*." This means, with great effort, you are to drive yourself toward God. Fight to pray. Fight to study the Word of God. Fight to keep your mouth shut and never be critical. Also, keep your hearing closed and do not listen to the negative. Then, labor to enter into that rest. Hunger and thirst after God with all of your heart. Remember, righteousness is not an experience, it is a Person. You're only as righteous as He is righteous in you. You must drive yourself toward Christ with all of your heart.

Now, let's look again in Isaiah at the price Christ paid that we might have eternal salvation. The redemption of our sins was fully settled on the cross. Always remember that for Jesus, the path to the cross began in the manger. He made His transition one step at a time, until He was led into the water of the Jordan River and was baptized by the Spirit of God. Then, His path of holiness brought Him face to face with encounters of miracles. These were just flowers planted along the pathway of His ultimate goal: the Cross. The Ministry of Christ was His coming into this world to be crucified. He who knew no sin became sin for us. He understood that it would take the breaking of His Flesh, the soul of the man in which He had come to live. He knew that it had to be conquered, that He might bear our sins in His Body on the tree, having been sinless in Himself.

Now, let's continue to look at His life and the transition of the conquering of that flesh, that we might, through Him, reign with Christ immortal. *Isaiah 53:7* states, "*He was oppressed and was afflicted, yet He opened not His mouth.*" One of the major signs of breaking, and of Christian maturity, is when the believer does not choose to defend himself to other people. When a Christian comes face to face with an issue, (an attack upon his character or life) anger is not ignited in the defense of himself. But within, that individual will begin to offensively attack his own emotional feelings in praise, until his anger is consumed by peace, and righteousness is rekindled in the heart. At that point, the attack no longer matters, for all that is truly important is a righteous relationship with God. You see, when you begin to defend yourself, you're reacting from an area of pride. To be misunderstood is one of the main postures that a walking-in-the-spirit-Christian must face in praise. Satan works upon your emotions to develop insecurity, which is the door to inferiority, a destruction of the Christian walk. Fear is the opposite of faith. A believer operating in the flesh will move to the volatile place of anger and try to defend himself. Do not do this. Use praise as a sword to free yourself from that demonic bondage. Remember, if you walk with God and are Holy Spirit led, you will be misunderstood. You are in a world system that hates God, and Satan will do all he can to get you from a position of brokenness or praise, back into flesh. He has to, for you are very dangerous to him when you praise. The simple reason is that a broken person is not only sufficient in Christ, but proficient in ministry. When I say "ministry," I mean the real thing. Not in the activity of religion, but the activity of the Holy Spirit, doing the Will of the Father, through the life of a joyful, broken Christian.

A. W. Tozer says: "Our Lord died an apparent failure, discredited by the leaders of established religion, rejected by society, and forsaken by His friends. The man who ordered Him to the cross was the successful statesman whose hand the ambitious hack-politician kissed. It took the Resurrection to demonstrate how gloriously Christ had triumphed and how tragically the governor had failed."

Some time ago, my whole family was placed into what we knew to be to us a tragic situation. For several years, we did not understand the reasons for that circumstance. But it was the beginning of the ministry that we have today. Our lives, our direction, and all that God had placed in us to do, had been misunderstood. Before it was all over with, there were deep hurts in every member of our household. Those that were closest to us, but not living with us in family, became very angry and hostile at what was being said and done. How desperately I wanted to defend myself! But God would not allow it.

It all started when I began to question the Pastor of a church in which I had ministered. I had preached a week long revival, resulting in a number of salvation decisions. When I contacted the pastor later, the Church body seemingly was in the same condition of coldness as it was before we came. Only a few of those born again would follow through with their commitments. After a decade of seeing decisions but no commitments in these revivals, I began to ask God to do whatever it took in my life to break me. I had to know that when I left a Church body after a revival, God's Kingdom would advance. I made this a matter of constant prayer. When God began the breaking of my life, I did not immediately realize what was happening. He was literally answering my prayers by first attacking my pride in the areas of my reputation and ministry. I had spent a lifetime building a good name and trying to develop a trusting relationship with pastors. In fact, it was with great conceit that I could say that where I had been in meetings, for the most part, the church wanted me back.

Now, I had lost face with my own pastor because of the directions in prayer I had received. The next thing we knew, the entire church was aware of our position because the pastor had made statements regarding our ministry from the pulpit. The very thing that I had guarded the most, and had been most important, was suddenly yanked out of my testimony in an instant. How we grieved! How we wept! How my family sorrowed as they sought reasoning from me as to what had happened. During that time, my young teenage son, in tears, asked me why all of his friends from church would no longer speak to him. I mourned over this more than all of the other circumstances that had come to pass. The situation had not only affected me, but also my family. Satan had a field day with his accusations. Why God? Why? What have I done to deserve this?

I asked the Lord to allow me to straighten-out this matter. But I could hear nothing in my spirit. Soon, my pastor's stand against me swept across the convention in which I was working. Now, those friends that knew me and trusted my ministry were suddenly doubting that our message was validly from God. Satan constantly bombarded my mind with, "Defend yourself." Yet, every time I would start to do it, God would speak to my spirit and say, "No, keep your mouth shut; this is for your good and My Glory."

So, for several years, we walked in that darkness of being misunderstood. Yet miraculously God supplied meetings, ministry, and His wonderful grace through that dark period. It was the hardest experience I had ever faced in my life. Today, I realize what it was all about. In my flesh, I wanted desperately to defend my position. I wanted to continue to be received for who I was at the level I had worked so hard to obtain. Pride. How strong its pull to our nature! It is the most powerful door to our emotions. Satan, as the past-master, holds the key to make it work. We must, with all effort, attack in praise and destroy its hold on our lives. We must.

Beloved, out of those years of brokenness, and asking why, was birthed a wonderful ministry that we had never before experienced. Today, as I look back upon it, I understand the reason God made it happen. I praise Him for the astounding life changing events, along with the constant sufficiency of His Grace. For without it, we would not be witnessing the dimension of glory or ministry that we are today. I do not, for an instant, believe I have "arrived" or attained, but I am in a totally different place of prayer, knowing His peace more than I have ever known. With great joy, I know that we are definitely pointed in the right direction for His Ministry through us. It is wonderful and it's just the beginning!

OUR PATTERN FOR BROKENNESS

In *Isaiah 53:7*, we find Christ's own experience of brokenness.

"He was oppressed and He was afflicted, yet He opened not His mouth. He is brought as a lamb to the slaughter and as a sheep before the shearers is dumb, so he opened not His mouth."

This Scripture gives us insight to the awesome price that Christ was to pay upon the cross, as well as in His itinerant ministry here upon this earth. He would, because of His Life, make full proof of His origin. We also find that He would be despised and rejected of men. But lest we miss the true message given here for us, it must be understood that He:

"for the joy of obtaining the prize that sat before Him -- endured the cross, despising and ignoring the shame, and is now seated at the right hand of the throne of God," *(Hebrews 12:2b, Amplified).*

However, the trials that He faced while here upon this earth cannot be looked at in a natural form or way. It must be remembered that He was the very Son of God, with the emotion of purity so clear within that there was a complete abhorrence of sin. For He who knew no sin became sin for us, that we who are conceived in sin might have forgiveness of our sins. Then, through the atonement or "at-one-ment" of being at-one with Christ, we might be redeemed. We, however, shall not know until we get home what our Lord truly went through in His life here upon this earth. Not only did He face separation from the Father and His presence in heaven, but He was bound into a system of religious laws that totally opposed and rejected all that He was as He walked here upon this earth. Unfortunately, it continues to be that way today, (*Romans 8:7*).

But perhaps the greatest burden of brokenness that He bore in His earthly ministry was the compassion He felt for the people. In one Scripture reference, we are given an insight into His true feelings. *Matthew 9:36* shares:

"When He saw the multitudes, He was moved with compassion on them because they fainted

and were scattered abroad as sheep having no shepherd."

Now, the word "concern" would be more understandable in the norm of today's religions. Many times we have become involved in ministering to the hungry because we have seen the need, whether the need was missions at home or overseas. In regard to Christ, however, the word "compassion" in that verse could be described as "the agony of the soul". He saw the need and bore its burden within. How desperately we need to see the world through the eyes of Christ. Oh, God, break us that we can have revival.

Again, we must understand that although He had the body of a human, because of constant prayer, He also had the transformed sensitivity and feelings of God, because he was deeply and intensely moved and broken. He wept "bitter tears" over the multitudes. He sobbed over their hunger, their hurts, and their needs. As was God, who "*so loved the world that He gave His only begotten Son,*" manifested that same love through the life of the Messiah as He was face to face with the desolate hearts and needs of the people. This was not only in caring for their spiritual needs, but even for their physical needs, as we find in *Matthew 15:32*. The crowds had been with Him for three days and would not leave for fear of missing the message and miracles of God through His Son. In this verse we receive an insight of what God feels for the human, as He, in the flesh, became overwhelmed and broken with the physical needs of these people. From that place of compassion, God provided through the prayer of Jesus, the miracle of the loaves and fishes. There were provisions for five thousand men, plus women and children. When the meal was over, He commanded that the remainder of the food be picked up. The leftovers, when gathered, were twelve baskets full. This was the result of God's Will and Christ's Faith. He first was moved with compassion for their need. Then He prayed, (blessed) the food, and the Father through Him supplied the need, (*Matthew 14:17-21*). Incidentally, compassion is the key to all true praying.

One of the major signs of being broken before the Lord, and filled with His Presence, is that you see what He sees and you feel what He feels. It is not you. It is Christ in you. Your heart is overwhelmed to give, or to serve, far beyond your own personal capacity and desires. From that experience the Christian is birthed into a pure ministry of God as the Holy Spirit takes control.

Recently, ministering in the Philippines, I felt a deep burden for the needs of those wonderful people. First, for their salvation, and secondly, that they would grow in grace through the Word so that they could learn to pray and walk as led by the Holy Spirit. A breaking has occurred in my own being several times while ministering there. During this breaking I would teach the pastors about prayer and brokenness, so that they might instruct their own churches on hearing from God. I could not hinder the tears from flowing. I was totally over-whelmed by the spiritual needs of this great nation, and yet I knew it was not me, but the Holy Spirit within me who was loving them. I might add here that this is the result of weeks of praying before we left on the journey. We could, through a burden, experience in a very small way what He was feeling for His precious Filipinos.

There have been moments in my life when I've experienced that compassion. I regard those times as inestimable, for I recognize that what had happened to me is that I had traded my emotions for His. For in those times and under the control of the Spirit, we spoke His Word, not only with authority and with power, but also with Glory as His Spirit would break upon the hearts of the listeners. And, Beloved, I knew all the time, full well, that I had nothing to do with the endeavor, especially the marvelous victories that were and are always present in these kinds of experiences.

My friend, of the thirty-five years of evangelism, these have been the greatest moments of my life. They have brought the most profound fruits and results. As I recall in every time of victory, however, I was experiencing some form of brokenness. While in that period of tribulation, I could do nothing but abandon myself to the Lord in prayer. It resulted in a great fear in my heart that the people would receive my ministry rather than God's. I would beg Him to break me, to speak through me. The results were always a pure vehicle of His Will.

Oh, precious, wonderful moments of grace! How wondrous the experience of walking with God and knowing you had nothing to do with the event. All of those times are eternal in purpose, and blessed in memory. But to have this, you must labor to bring yourselves into that place of breaking. This was the Ministry of Christ here upon this earth, that in His own heart through breaking, He had desperate compassion for the people. It must happen to us so that He can continue to be an instrument of God's Grace.

Now, we find in *Hebrews 5:7*:

"... while He was alive in the days of His flesh, He offered up prayers and supplication, with strong crying and tears unto Him that was able to save Him from death and was heard in that He feared."

When you search the depths of that verse, there is a phrase that establishes the walk with God in true relationship with His Will. Jesus, in prayer, cried before His Father with a broken heart. The key to it all is best explained in the Amplified:

> *"And He was heard because of His reverence toward God. His Godly fear, His piety. That is in that He shrank from the horrors of separation, from the bright presence of the Father."*

What divine explanation of Christ's, walk with God! Yours is to be the same.

Jesus as God incarnate constantly controlled His feelings and His flesh in order to retain or maintain an abiding relationship with the Father. Christians should do identically the same in prayer, driving themselves toward the Lord and thereby practicing the presence of God in their lives. We must battle against the flesh.

Before we leave this place, let's look once more at the statement in *Hebrews 5:7*: *"... in that He shrank from the horrors of separation, from the bright presence of the Father."* Words have never stated so clearly the truth of our walk with God. It is a struggle to bring the flesh into control. Satan hinders any effort in the life of a Christian who has come through the doors of tribulation into the *"bright presence"* of God's Glory, Peace, and place in his heart. He must dim the light. He must block our memory of the moments of grace, and the preciousness of the relationship of the Holy Spirit's control of our lives. He must, by every form, create crises of anger, depression, reaction, division, and negative confession. Satan must, by diversionary action, "snatch the seed" and make us forget.

I believe all of satanic dominion is stirred into battle when Christians, in brokenness, come into the Light and begin to enjoy the wondrous presence of God in their hearts. I also accept the Scripture that says that demonic princes are called into engagement to hinder, (*I Thessalonians 2:18*). In the state of contriteness, the Christian is most dangerous to the demon-world system of principalities. It is in penitence that these Christians are listening to God. They are walking in the Spirit. He is ministering His will to them, and through them. In that trial, their affections are changing them from the flesh to the Spirit. The truth is, we should seek and so walk with Jesus, that even the thought of separation would be such a horror to our lives that we would fight in prayer to maintain the relationship.

My beloved friends, this fight in prayer is imperative to the Christian walk. That's why we must pray to be broken. We must believe and act upon it in faith so that God will move into our lives and conform us to the image of His dear Son, that ours would be as the cry of Paul as he said in *Philippians 3:10*:

> *"That I may know Him and the power of His resurrection and the fellowship of His sufferings, being made conformable to His death."*

For it is through the door of glorious suffering that we are birthed into the true life and Will of God, coming to that which has been laid out for us before history began, (*Ephesians 2:10*).

GAMES PEOPLE PLAY

In another area of Christ's Ministry, we find the shortest verse in the Bible. *"Jesus wept,"* (*John 11:35*). In examining the circumstances, we see that at Lazarus' grave, His tears flowed. Such was the brokenness and compassion upon Him at that moment. In fact, those who had stood around the grave site as paid mourners, were suddenly quieted as they observed His weeping. Christ was so overcome they said of Him, "**Lo, how He loved him.**" Jesus was not, however, lamenting for a four-day old dead body and the loss of a friend. He knew that in a moment He would speak. The physical would again come alive, well and restored from that grave site, with his spirit married again to the flesh that had already become putrid from death. For all He would have to say is, "Lazarus, come forth," and, by the Power of God, he would.

You say then, "Why was Christ sobbing in such a broken state?" It is my personal belief after study that in this case people play games called "religion". They take a Biblical precedent and pursue it and say, "Because I work at this with great and extreme effort, by the laws of my particular faith, I am full of grace." From this concept, as I stated previously, there is estimated to be over 20,000 Christian denominations in the world and all of them are Biblically right in their own eyes. Also, they all get their so-called revelation of the true path to righteousness from the same book, the Bible.

No, dear friend, Jesus was not weeping for the man that He knew He would have fellowship with in a few moments. I personally believe that He was broken over the sham and the lost condition of the paid mourners who were falsely wailing at the loss of Lazarus. He was broken over their unreality. For His compassion is toward the living. The dead can "**bury the dead,**" the Scripture says. Jesus knew the hearts of those who were there and the game they were playing. Oh, how He wept! Broken over the games people still play. They trade principles for the Person of Christ; religion for righteousness.

If but one individual in a church, seeing what God sees in the theological compromises, then feeling what God feels about the players involved, would be moved with compassion and broken over that congregation, and would then, in that contrite state, begin to fast and pray, the results would not only bring about Biblical reality, but would birth revival. If just ONE would see! (*Isaiah 59:16*)

Oh, my dear friend, it is imperative that we have a visitation from God upon this earth now. However, it will never come in what we're doing. It can only be birthed through a broken, contrite, and abandoned heart. In that position, the heart sees what God sees, (**II Chronicles 7:14**). As Jesus wept and prayed for those around Him, God came into the midst to heal, to deliver, to save, and to feed. God will be moved in this day only through broken contrite prayer. We must have the Power of Christ through us for all this to happen. We must see what He sees. We can. We must!

I beg you to present your body as a living sacrifice back to God. Then walk daily in Him by taking authority over the flesh and giving your life back to Him. The results of that wonderful relationship will be a great horror at the thought of breaking that fellowship. If you live in the magnitude of His Grace, you will become used to His Glory, and will continually desire it. Again, you must be broken before the Lord, (*Isaiah 57:15, 66:2*).

Before we continue to more truths, let's take one final look at the reason God came to this earth clothed in the body of a man. So much has been written about the doctrine of the transformed life, and yet so little is understood about it. Christianity in its present form is bound by the concepts or precepts of men. They organize religion, developing levels of righteousness through religious activities.   It is just as communism. In its original belief and ideology, its purpose was to bring utopia to the world, as big brother would take control of all assets and minister to the needs of the people. In its dogma, by law all must work, and all would be rewarded. The only problem was that it had no place for God in the spirit being of the man. Man is designed by God with a spirit in order to know God and be in union with Him. Therefore, as communism is, so is religion. For the most part, it has no place for the Spirit of God to fill the spirit of man. Satan desires the world to believe that mankind is an evolutionary, animal-like being, with no need or consciousness of a Holy God and Creator.

Again, Bible-based religion is man-based activities, being performed by Christians. When, through prayer, the heart of God comes in our tribulation, He becomes our only hope of Glory. From that experience, as long as the Holy Spirit is in control, we move to a completely different level of thinking and lifestyle. For "*our thoughts are not His thoughts*," except when we're consumed by His Mind, (*Philippians 2:5*). So, in actuality, the transformed life is Christ living through us according to His Will, (*Romans 12:1-2*). Beloved, that is the greatest experience; for it is the beginning of ALL ministry. Again, it enters only through the door of brokenness. When we have yielded our lives to Him, in complete and total abandonment through the gate of tribulation, we stand ready for Him to extend His Life through us. These are the greatest experiences of Christian life!

Let's look now at the final breaking of our Lord as He prepared to take our sins in His Body on the Tree. Jesus Christ, in our redemption, was taken through the greatest persecution that any mortal has ever experienced. It must be remembered that He had a human body. Immortality put on mortality that we might, through Him, have eternal life. Upon completion of His torture by the soldiers and His time on the Cross, the Scripture says, "*His visage was marred more than any man.*" No living human being in history has ever looked like Jesus did that day. The Satan-led demonic forces in the purest of hate, through the hands of men, did all they could to bring death upon the body of the Son of God, (*I Corinthians 2:7-8*). A crown of thorns was placed on His head as a symbol of His Kingliness. The guards bowed down and worshipped Him in mockery. Then, He was beaten over His head with a reed, very likely used to prod the cattle, (for He was at "gabatha", or the pavement where the animals were kept). After that, He was whipped. This whip was not a Jewish scourge, but that of a Roman. It was an instrument of war. It usually contained lead balls at the end of each strand of leather. When brought down with great force, it could crush the head of a man. With it, the Romans flogged Jesus until He was an open wound. Always remember, He had a human body. He came as God wrapped in human flesh. In fact, He was "*God with us*."

The Bible continues by saying that they doubled up their fists and beat Him. The Greek word used here is "buffeted." In a wild frenzy, these burly guards battered Him as they were filled with hatred beyond description. They were led by Satan's attempt to rid the world of its Messiah. Then, one of those men took His beard and jerked it out of His face. They continued to beat Him and beat Him. Finally, it was over. Jesus, in His thrashed state, bleeding profusely, and swollen beyond recognition as a human being, was presented to Pilate for crucifixion.

"Religion" sent Jesus to the cross. My beloved, it hates all that is anointed of God. The same hatred is evident toward pure Christianity, as we will see in these end times. We will actually be despised for His Name's sake. Pilate would have let Christ go free, but the religious leaders wanted Him crucified and out of the way, because Jesus was revealing the truth about the condition of the church as it was. Again, as *Romans 8:7* teaches, there is no common ground between pure Christianity and the works of the flesh through religious activity in today's church. The Bible declares, "*it is enmity to God*." The word "enmity" in the Greek means "hostile". Most people do not want anything to do with the True and Living God in their churches. How well the Scripture says of the religions of today, "*They have a form of Godliness, but deny the power thereof.*" That does not mean they dispute the blood atonement, the resurrection, and the second coming of Jesus Christ. It means that they reject the sovereign position of the Spirit of God controlling their hearts and lives. Everyone wants a Savior, but no one wants a Lord. Be assured however, that He is, and ever shall be, LORD!

Jesus was then led away, crippled in flesh. Again, His body was that of a human, having put the garment of flesh upon His body of Spirit, that He might be subject to the like things that we are. Yet, standing against them in God and through prayer, Jesus made a way of escape for us. Oh, how He loved us! Beloved, it is impossible to understand this in our finite minds. The moment that we, as children of God, leave this life, either through physical death or by rapture, our spirits will escape our bodies and will be instantly in the presence of God. We will at once see Jesus as He really is. And immediately, in that glorified state of mind, we will know what was done for us through Jesus' Life upon this earth and through the work of the Cross of Calvary. At that wondrous moment, we, who are born again, will crumble at His feet in honor and in praise, and we shall glorify His name and shall cry with others:

> "*Blessing and honor and glory and power be unto Him that sitteth upon the throne, and unto the Lamb for ever and ever,*" (*Revelation 5:13*).

We shall truly know how great our God is! How wonderful is His love for us, that He gave us Jesus Christ!

Praise the Lord in Glory! Praise Him! *"How excellent is Thy Name, O Lord!"*

Lest we forget, we are studying the reason for breaking of God in the Flesh, for our redemption. They laid upon Him the cross to carry, and in His physically weakened state, He could not stand up and fell beneath its load. The Roman guards had complete, sovereign authority over this captured nation, and commanded a man named Simon, from Cyerene, to then bear His cross to Calvary's hill.

There, they nailed Him to the tree, and as they raised the cross, it slid into the hole. It tore at everything in His body. Have you ever wondered, in looking at pictures of crucifixions, why the knees of those crucified were always bent? The reason is so that the person could inhale air to keep his body alive. But he could not exhale. As he became weaker and his body began to pull at his arms with its weight, the bones around the neck would begin to close. The arms would have to pull up the body, the legs supporting the weight as long as possible, in order to open that air passage to exhale air.

Jesus hung naked upon that cross, fighting for life and breath, yet His Mission, based on His Commission, had not yet been accomplished. It was not yet finished. Remember, Christ had come to this world to bear our sins in His Body on the tree. For hours He was in agony, fighting for life and breath. The Scripture gives us a picture of what He went through on the Cross. But, my beloved friend, only when we get home will we truly see the totality of the price He paid for us. It shall overwhelm us. We shall cry, and cry, and cry, *"Worthy is the Lamb that was slain. Worthy."*

And then, suddenly, terror gripped the hearts of that assembled crowd, as the sky grew dark. The earth began to shake with great tremor. The greatest event in all human history had progressed to its main event within this three-day period. At that moment, the whole planet began to react physically to its creator because God, who knew no sin, and could not look upon sin, made His Son to become sin, that we might have everlasting life. For it was then that He turned His back upon Jesus, and the Earth responded with quaking. Perhaps the universe also. We will know when we get home someday.

WHAT LOVE

At the time of crucifixion, the sins of Adam and Eve were stabbed into the very person of the Son of God. Penetrating into His Spirit was the first murder, as He took the sins of Cain, who killed his brother, Abel. On and on through the pages of history, as through the first thousand years, the sins of every human being were put on Jesus as He became sin for them. I believe He knew them all by name. Then, all the way to the flood, where in history's darkest hour to that moment, God destroyed the world's system the first time and only eight people were saved. The total iniquities of all humanity to that place in history coursed through the life of Jesus Christ as He hung on the cross in utter agony. He who knew no sin became sin for them.

The sins of every human being continued to be discharged as the ages passed. His crucifixion crashed the barriers of time as His blood covered the sins of every man, woman, and child, including those who have not yet been born. He bore our sins in His Body on the tree. Again, when Christ died upon the cross, He took the sins of all, and beloved, His death was sufficient.

It is desperately important to note here one thing in the avenue of His brokenness for our eternal redemption. During

His walk upon this earth, He cherished a constant relationship with His Father the most. Prayer was His life-line from which to regress, and to face existence in this world system. It was truly His spiritual umbilical. Therefore, in His aloneness, He unceasingly "called home." He constantly went apart to pray. It is written that He was in perpetual contact and oneness with the Father. He truly was a personification of the verse that says we are to *pray without ceasing*." But suddenly, God, who could not look upon sin, who made His Son to be sin for us, closed off that relationship of His presence and communication. For the next three hours, with indescribable agony and abandonment, so far beyond the description of words or concept of mind, the Son of God bore our sins in His Body on the tree.

> "No words in human language,
> No thoughts in human mind,
> No prose in human writing,
> Could search the truth of the Divine."

Jesus sobbed in anguish at the loss of the presence of His "*Abba*," Daddy. He cried, *My God, my God, why has Thou forsaken me?*" It is no wonder the Earth became enveloped in darkness, trembling at its foundation from an earthquake. At that moment it totally yielded and convulsed, feeling the agony of its maker. He had formed with His mouth and spoken into being all that was, for all that was made was made by Jesus Christ, (*Colossians 1:16*).

Hanging there, His strength and blood continued to ebb from His Body as He pulled Himself against the nails with His arms and pushed Himself with His feet to be able to breathe and to hold onto life. He will remain alive long enough to redeem every human being in history by the scarlet life of His veins. He must. HE MUST! Oh, the Precious Lamb of God, who was taken to His cross, opened not His mouth, as a sheep that before her shearers is dumb, (*Isaiah 53:7*).

The Scripture gives us one final look at His visage, or what He looked like hanging on the cross. It tells us in *Psalm 22:14* that He literally became "***poured out like water***." Every bone came out of joint, every tendon, every ligament. Every muscle stretched as the weight of His body caused it to sag to its limits, until the nerves screamed in agony. Oh, how simple it would have been to give up and go home, or to call the angels to minister to Him! However, it could not be done, for His work was not yet finished. The sins of the whole human race had to be paid for. So, with effort beyond our finite understanding, Jesus Christ fought to hold onto His life in that human body, in order to bear our sins. He held on, and on, and on. Oh, God in Glory, how worthy is the Lamb! How worthy to be praised!

Darkness draped about all who stayed. It was mingled only with the sounds of a struggling body gasping for air, and the scraping of broken flesh upon the cross as He forced Himself up, only to fall back as His weight could not be sustained by trembling weakened muscles. He had to hold on to life. He had to. It was not finished yet. Oh, what Love! But the suffering inside Him was far beyond the description of His external pain. Like the pouring of scalded water upon an infant child, our sins were, circulating through His Body. He bore them all, <u>All</u>, from the beginning of history to the very end. And yet, these words, in description of His Mission, seem too simple in their expression. However, the closest to explaining this truth is when God says, "***He bore our sins in His Body on the tree,***" (*I Peter 2:24*). Affliction beyond description, and again, oh, what love!

This most important event in all of history was finally coming to its completion and close. Jesus, fighting to hold on to life as the pain of His body mingled with the wretchedness of our sins, also fought a battle to retain life until the mission of His Coming was accomplished. Finally, all that could be done to Him was done. It was over. He fought physically to remain until the price was paid. It had to be done. The last sin had to be consumed and canceled by His blood.

Now, Satan, who operates in death, felt he had finally won the victory, (*I Corinthians 2:7-8*). To him, God was dying. Jesus was being conquered in the eyes of the devil. It was his last opportunity to win, and he felt he had been victorious. But without his knowledge, something wondrously unique was happening. We will cast our crowns at Christ's feet when we get home someday because of this event. To understand what He went through with our finite minds, we must know the reason for His life in its miraculous birth, in its living, and in its union with God by the Spirit, at His baptism in the Jordan River. The purpose of the miracles, all the way to His death on the cross, was for our eternal salvation. In fact, the agony of the last hours of His life can best be explained by how He held onto His physical existence for our redemption. Please remember, He spoke of Himself constantly as the Son of Man. That meant that His God qualities were married to the weaknesses of the flesh. That's why He constantly went apart to pray, keeping His focus totally upon God, and the Spirit of the Living Father ministering through Him the Power of His Will. He conquered His flesh. It is totally indescribable to understand what that means to us in this life. But, God will reveal the hidden things.

Now, as we found earlier in *John 5*, Jesus stated of Himself that His Ministry was that of the Father through Him. When Christ is alive in us, that same ministry exists. It is *"Christ in you, the hope of glory."* This comes only by and through answered prayer.

Then Christ, from the cross cried, "*It is finished*." And it was. Every sin had been covered by His Blood. Every human in history could now look upon Him in His death and resurrection in faith, believing in the Lord Jesus Christ, and from that moment on, through faith and broken confession of sins, receive Him as their Savior. From the instant of His death on the cross came redemption. Redemption was for all, from the beginning of human history, to the last person who shall ever live. Anyone who will believe, repent, confess his sins, and ask Christ to save him will find the old redemption story, and gain the promise of everlasting life; for the purpose of the cross is found in *Romans 14:9*, *"for to this end Christ both died and rose, and revived, that he might be Lord both of the dead and living."*

Also in *II Corinthians 5:15* He stated, *"and that he died for all, that they which live should not henceforth live unto themselves, but unto him which died for them and rose again."* How great our God and His Christ!

By now, the crowd on Calvary's hill was gone. Just a few who loved Him remained at the cross. The guards were ready to leave the area because too many strange things had happened that day. Yet they knew not to run as the crowd did. Roman law stated that if the person being crucified was seen alive after his crucifixion, those in charge would have to take his place. These men were very careful to make sure that death had found its victory in the three that were nailed to the tree that day.

They approached the first of those three men. Very likely, he was still alive, and became the first to find death at the point of a spear, after the pain of the breaking of the legs, as was the law. When they came to Jesus, they looked at Him. Remember, the Scripture says literally, that no human being in history had ever looked like Christ looked upon the cross. "*He was poured out like water*." Every bone was out of joint. His body was swollen from beatings. His head, perhaps as one physician said, was so bruised that it could have been very close to being distended to twice its normal size. His lips were protruding and expanded from the beating. "*His tongue cleaved to the roof of His mouth*." So close to death by shock was He in His human body! Such was His "*visage*," or outward appearance.

So they knew, being Roman soldiers of occupation, and through perhaps many crucifixions, that this One was already dead. Therefore, at random, they threw the spear and instead of piercing below the breastbone and going through the heart, they penetrated His side and, "*water and blood flowed and mingled down*." There has been much theory about this, but it is my personal feeling, after study, that the reason there was water and blood gathered above the bowels where they pierced, was because of another part of the Miracle of Christ upon the cross. From what I understand, if you are a normal human being, around your heart God has placed a water sac which acts as a shock absorber. If someone hits you in the chest or some accidental bruising comes, that liquid helps to keep this vital organ from being bruised or harmed, so that death might not occur from the event.

I would ask you to consider this, based on the love our Christ had for us. As He hung upon the cross, He held on and held on to His life. Regarding this, I have heard many stories over the years about individuals who were very close to death, yet fought to retain their lives until the one whom they deeply loved was able to come. After seeing that loved one a last time, the people slipped into eternity. So I believe it was with Christ, as He hung upon the cross for our sins. Such was His Love for us, that until all was paid, He held onto the body functions as

He gripped life. When anyone should have died perhaps from the beatings, or from the first moments upon the cross, Jesus remained alive until the last human in history had his sins redeemed and cleansed by His Blood. OH, WHAT LOVE!

When the purchase price for our redemption was finally paid and all was sufficient, the overwhelming pressure of the shock of sin and the pain of His body, plus the loss of relationship with His Father that brought agony to the soul, caused the heart to begin to swell by great pressure. This has been known of runners who have given their all until finally collapsing. Their hearts physically burst, having run the race with the most extreme effort of their lives. I believe such was the case with Jesus. He held on and on until all of our sins were redeemed. He would not let go until our redemption was finished. At the moment it was finished, He moved back to the true condition of His body, and His heart physically burst. My Beloved, I believe He died of a broken heart for you and me. Oh, wondrous Savior! Oh, gracious Lord! "Greater Love hath no man...."

It shattered for you and me. Then when they pierced His side, and water and blood mingled, flowing down, it was, I believe, the blood and water from a pure but broken heart that had collected over the bowel. In the light of this, is it any wonder what our reaction shall be when we get home some day, and we will in glorified mind, truly see Him as He is, based on who we are and what He has done for us. All Hail the POWER OF JESUS' NAME!

F. B. Meyer wrote:

"This is the key to the incarnation. With slight alternation, the words will read truly of that supreme act. He rose from the throne; laid aside the garments of light which He had worn as His vesture; took up the poor towel of humanity, and wrapped it about His Glorious Person; poured His own Blood into the basin of the Cross; and set Himself to wash away the foul stains of human depravity and guilt.

As pride was the source of human sin, Christ provided an antidote in His absolute humility -- a humility which could not grow beneath these skies, but must be brought from the world where the lowliest are the greatest and the most childlike reign as kings."

Now do you understand? He says, "*This is my body, it is broken thereof.*" Do you comprehend? "*This is my cup, the cup of my blood thereof.*" Can you see the price that was paid for our redemption? He was broken, bruised and beaten that we might be born again and blessed, not only in this world, but for all eternity. My precious, beloved friends:

> "*He was wounded for our transgressions. He was bruised for our iniquities. The chastisement of our peace was upon Him and with His stripes we are healed.*" (*Isaiah 53:5*)

It is as the hymn writer of old stated in the song:

> "Jesus paid it all,
> All to Him I owe.
> Sin has left a crimson stain,
> He washed it white as snow."

The ultimate example of all breaking was the Son of God. Would we so pray for that event in our lives and have the joyous presence of His Glory upon us and the wondrous walk of faith as we yield our lives to Him? Brokenness! Blessed, hallowed brokenness! It is truly the road to victory and the hidden factor to the Will of God. Pray to be broken. Seek Him with all of your heart. Learn the joyous experience of His Glory upon your life. Worthy is the Lamb! WORTHY!

CHAPTER FIVE

ROUND AND ROUND SHE GOES

I have, in these thirty-five years as an itinerant evangelist, experienced moments of wondrous joy. These have been occasions when the Holy Spirit has moved mightily across the ministry of the church in which I was involved. I would bask in these seasons by using them in other churches as illustrations of God's Power, thereby wetting their spiritual appetites to experience the same. I wanted to express to them that revival could come if they would pay the price. Then I would reflect back to the "why's" of the outpouring of God's Spirit at that particular time, and would be reminded that those periods were an overflow of God's Grace to my life in the midst of a tribulation in which I was presently experiencing.

I often stated that if there was no revival or move of God in a meeting, it was the fault of the people for not preparing by prayer and activity. On the other hand, if God did move in power, I would strongly accentuate the miracles of God as a credit to my abilities to preach. Because of this, I was brought to a more profound wilderness experience, as God would not share His Glory with me. Then I would, again, see my ministry in a dry and desolate place. In the process of this cycle, there would be a returning to God with tears. This would restore the Anointing and Presence of His Glory. For only through brokenness would come the glorious visitation of Christ's Life that produced great results, His results. Satan, however would convince my pride that the effects of God's workings were a result of my own abilities. I would once more plummet into the abyss of separation as he would whisper in my ear, "Look what you're doing for God." How many times I have been around that mountain! Denney expressed my plight best as he wrote, "You can't, in preaching, produce at the same time the impression that you are clever and that Christ is wonderful." How tragically slow we learn to discern that it is Jesus only and nothing else. Paul stated it best, "*Oh wretched man that I am*."

Please beloved, I beg you, in these trying and perilous times, to submit totally to God's Spirit and Life through you. It has to happen. Nothing eternal shall be accomplished until Christ does it through you. You must learn quickly the lesson of brokenness and His abundant flow through the cracks in your "earthen vessel."

As I said earlier, I have been a student of revival the entire period of my ministry, and have begged for His visitation in and through my life. I once desired to learn all the "methods" of ministry, that I might be able to see the Glory of God upon the hearts of men through salvation and transformation! I copied the ministries of successful men through my labor of works, only to find that what had been blessed of God for them did not work in my ministry. It was just not to be for me, except for short seasons and events that were the results of my being broken before the Lord.

Then, once more, as victories came, I began to forget why God had blessed in those times. It is like a woman stating at the moment of giving birth, "I'll never do this again." The blessing of carrying a precious life for those months is forgotten in the time of great pain and fear. But when the newborn is brought into the presence of the mother, suddenly joy is wrapped in the arms of the love of motherhood. This new experience soon wipes away the memory of the tribulation suffered, and one day life is once again formed within the body. Another is on the way!

HEROES

In search of greater power, I would read of the life of Jonathan Edwards who, though slight of stature and nearly blind, had such anointing upon his life that as he preached, men would hold onto the pews to keep from falling into hell. Oh, to experience that in ministry! So I attempted, in part, his message, "Sinners in the hand of an angry God," thinking that surely the Power was in my ability to preach and not just in the manifestation of the Spirit. I so desired to have that kind of significance and authority that would cause men to tremble before God. That would really make my ministry take off, and I could get into the bigger churches and, wonder of wonders, even have an organization like Billy Graham. "Here I come, Lord." But, it would not happen. When you really study the life of Edwards and understand, you will see that the secret of his being was in his prayerful, shameless, desperate love for Christ. All that transpired within and around him was the effect of a complete yieldedness and total dependency upon God, His life, and His Holy Spirit.

Charles Finney is another hero whose life results I have studied. His transcribed messages and personal writings have greatly inspired me. Oh, what power and glory upon this man! The results that came from the avenues of his testimony had their sources in heaven, and came flowing through him as he was in the presence of men! Such was the anointing upon him that, as he spoke, men's hearts would be struck in such brokenness! They would cry, as dying men, for repentance and the forgiveness of God! Oh, to be like Finney! Surely to preach his messages would bring that same glory. But again, it was not to be. Mr. Finney, an attorney, had so sought God in the desolation of his heart, that he held on in prayer until there was the filling of the Spirit in his life. He begged God to fill him, and would not leave that Presence of Prayer until it was done. As always, the results of a heart broken before God, brought the outpouring of the Spirit on his life in such profound proportions that he had to plead with the Lord to stay, lest he die. The Glory was so strong as it swept over his soul, (*Ephesians 5:18*). When he walked out of the woods where he had gone to seek God that day, such was the presence of God's Glory upon him. From that moment on it is said that people would tremble when he would walk into a room where they were assembled.

In fact, history states through writings about his life, that he was brought into a factory to observe its activity. Unknown to the people was this man who was totally yielded to the Lord. As he came through the door, a woman working on a machine looked up and saw his face. She fell to her knees and crumbled in the Presence of God, seeking forgiveness and repentance. Soon, the whole factory was crying out to God for salvation. Oh, to be like Finney. To have that Glory upon my life. It must have been his message. Surely this would also work for me as it did for him. It did not. It was like having an automobile with all of the equipment to make it go. Its design capabilities were there to take me anywhere, at maximum speed. However, it had no battery. There was no power to get it started. For the most part, such was my ministry. Ready to go anywhere, but no power.

I remember years ago having participated in a great move of God in a church, pastored by Jack Taylor in San Antonio, Texas. Our hearts were broken in joy as the people cried out for revival and the Spirit of God fell upon those members, consuming them. It was an experience I will remember for a lifetime. In that meeting was a man of faith by the name of Manley Beasley. Considering all the men of God that I had ever met, I held the very highest respect and regard for Manley Beasley. He was a man of deep faith, prayer, and power with

God. I sat with him for days in a hospital in Houston, Texas in the early '70s. The doctors reported that he had three terminal diseases and that he would never leave that place. While visiting him, I saw those whom I felt were giants of God come through that hospital door. They had known of his life, and had come to share moments of encouragement and prayer, as well as to say good-bye to a friend who was diagnosed not to leave that establishment alive.

One of those who visited was a woman by the name of Corrie Ten Boom. In the course of her conversation with Manley, she suddenly ceased what she was saying, raised her eyes to the ceiling and said, "Yes, Lord, if that's what you want me to do, I'll do it." She went back to talking to this man of God. Beloved, in all the years that have passed, I have never forgotten what happened when she looked up and agreed with God. At that moment, the room became filled with the Presence of the Glory of the Father. Later on, as I read the book written about her life, I discovered that the reason for this heavenly communication was that while in a German concentration camp, she had paid the price for that relationship. She was totally broken and was in joyous abandonment to God, in the midst of her confinement.

In regard to hearing from God, one day while praying, Manley asked the Lord, "What is going to happen to me?" In his weakened condition, God immediately called his attention to the verse, "***Thou shalt see thy children's children.***" Instantly he knew in the way God had spoken to his heart that he had a promise for his healing. In faith, he stood on the Word. Within a few weeks, he left that hospital with his doctors mystified as to his recovery. Because of that experience, there was a Glory upon him that was never present before. Later, as he spoke in the meeting we mentioned earlier, (in San Antonio, Texas), he had to be seated with a microphone on the platform because of his still weakened condition. As he quietly spoke, the Power of God surged through the hearts of everyone there, and because the church had prayed, revival broke out. Manley Beasley had paid a price. For the rest of his ministry, until he went home in the early 1990's, there was always a profound breaking in those who heard him. He paid the price.

Incidentally, after that brief encounter with Corrie Ten Boon in the hospital room, God allowed us several months later, to have thirty minutes alone with her to talk about the experiences she went through and where she was at that time with the Lord. I discovered again the walk she had was due to her power in prayer. As I have mentioned before, she had paid the price for that intimate relationship with the Lord. Such was the explanation of the Glory upon her ministry and life.

ANY OLD DONKEY WILL DO

Several times over these wonderful years of ministry, God has introduced me to places known for glorious revivals. For example, we had been a part of a number of meetings in Northern Ireland. Once, in a city on the Black River, which is the border for Ireland and Northern Ireland, we were ministering in a Presbyterian Church, teaching spiritual warfare praying. The pastor of that church and I were discussing a past move of God in that area. He knew my heart and he asked me if I would like to meet the couple who were with Duncan Campbell when the great revival broke out in the Hebrides. To the delight of my life, as that offer was made, I said "yes, oh yes". I had read and heard much of the stirring of God in the Hebrides and of Duncan Campbell, who was a renowned minister and evangelist who had lived in England.

The next day, we traveled to a city called Monihans, in Ireland, across the Black River and through the British checkpoints. We went to the home of a family in their mid-eighties by the name of Waters. It was a wonderful four hours of questions and answers. Upon leaving to get ready for the evening service at the church in Aughnacloy, the pastor invited this precious couple to come the next day to the Manse and have lunch. He promised them a proper tea if they would come. They were delighted and came to share even more in the memories of that astounding move of God.

One of the profound moments in my life was to take a cassette tape recorder and spend a full hour with Brother Waters, asking him questions of the miraculous events of God's Glory that fell on the Hebrides. When he was finished, Mrs. Waters came in, and I did the same thing with her, hoping to turn some fresh spade of the miracles of those experiences, as the fruit of the Spirit was planted, by prayer, in the soil of righteousness and sprouted into the life of revival.

In reviewing the interviews later, all that happened there shook down to one thing: broken vessels praying for God to intervene, (*Isaiah 57:15*). Prior to this time with the Waters, I had read of the Hebrides revival and the wonders that were so profound as God's Spirit moved across that land. Every bar was closed. Every house of prostitution ceased operation as its principals and participants burst into the Kingdom of God through the door of "salvation by grace through faith." History records, as well as their testimonies, that the revival was not because of the great preaching of Duncan Campbell. He denied having anything to do with it, even until his call home to heaven. In fact, I have on tape a very scratchy sermon that he preached toward the end of his life and ministry, demanding that people not place the results of that move upon him, but upon those who prayed the price to God. How tragic are the tendencies to credit the work of the Father to the names of men! Believe me, as I have experienced in my own life, it does not and will not work! There is room for only one Person on the Cross.

It is well said that "any old donkey will do," (*Numbers 22:23*). In fact, as I shared in a previous chapter, even the greatest of all Biblical servants, including Christ himself, had no form or comeliness. These servants were neither large and attractive physically, nor did they very likely have a presence of authority in their voices. One was nearly blind and bore no eloquence in his speech. Our Lord was described in *Isaiah 53:2* as being either typical or substandard physically, according to the size of the Jew of His day. The purpose of God, was to ensure that nothing be drawn to Jesus, the messenger, but only to His message, as was so profoundly spoken by the Spirit's authority through the mouth of God Incarnate, who had taken on the body of man. God became flesh and dwelt among men.

By Duncan Campbell's own testimony, as well as the Waters', the reason for the Hebrides revival can be wrapped up not in his oratory but because of a continuing prayer meeting in Stornoway and the lives of two women, one of whom was blind. They were sisters in their mid-eighties. They lived in a home behind the son of the sightless woman. Together their lives were spent with one joyful focus, and that was upon God, Prayer, and His Word. The testimony of all who knew them was that they prayed and wept unceasingly before the Lord, not just for revival in their church, but also for the anointed Glory of the Presence of God and His Power to fall upon the Hebrideans. They waited upon the Lord. They prayed. They, through intercession, were openly broken. God's Power was inevitable. That region of the world was so dark and away from God that its only hope was not for revival, but for a resurrection of God's Spirit in the hearts of people separated from God and His

Kingdom. It was as America and the world are today.

As God promises, the results are always the same when the conditions of *II Chronicles 7:14* are met. The first condition is to be humbled or broken. Secondly, we are to pray in desperate contriteness and humility. For, again, when we are contrite before the Lord, then we seek not our will but His. We are brought into His Presence only by the righteousness which is not ours, but is the level of Christ's control of our lives. It must be understood that we are only as righteous as He is righteous in us. That righteousness is developed only through the desperation within our hearts as we abandon our lives to Him, seeking Him with all of our might, demonstrating our need for Him. Once more, it is a total yielding to God, just as Job said, "*I demand of thee, declare thou unto me.*" In Stornoway men prayed for months for revival as they gathered in a little barn three nights a week. They interceded until 4 to 5 o'clock in the morning. They were determined to wrestle with God until He responded, (*Luke 18:1*). One evening a deacon stood and read *Psalm 24*::

> "*Who shall ascend into the hill of the Lord? or Who shall stand in His Holy Place? He that hath clean hands and a pure heart. He shall receive the blessings of the Lord.*"

He then asked the question of those assembled: "Are our hearts clean? Is the heart pure?" They begin to confess their sins and return in travail in prayer. Revival came upon them and the barn was filled with the Glory of God.

It was precisely the same time that morning that God spoke to the sisters (5 o'clock a.m.). As these women held onto the throne in contrite intercession, God caused the Hebrides to see Him. In that posture, God's promised Spirit fell upon them, and upon the entire country within days. A *Jeremiah 33:3* experience came upon these sisters one evening in prayer as they called upon God, and He answered. As a result of that event, they both rushed to the son's home to express what God had said, for He had declared to their spirits that revival would come. He promised that the Hebrideans would be brought into awakening and that His preaching instrument would be Duncan Campbell. Upon hearing this, the son, knowing the level of the walk of his mother and his aunt, began to noise abroad the promise they had received from the Lord. Opposition came very quickly by many in disbelief of the conditional events declared by these women. It was thought that there was no hope for the nation. The main cause of their rejection was the feeling that Duncan Campbell would never leave England and come to the Hebrides. But just in case, they made an attempt to contact him in the event that they had truly heard from God.

A message was sent to this man of God, whose crowds were large as his brilliant oratory, saturated with prayer, was blessed by God's Grace and Power. Upon receiving the information and an invitation to come to the Hebrides, he corresponded and stated his schedule had already been filled for the next two years. The word was sent back to the ladies stating that he could not come, for his calendar was fully booked. Then, the blind sister stated, "He'll be here in a fortnight," (two weeks). Such was the Presence of God in her life, and so great was the Word from God in her heart, that she knew he would come.

Several days later, in a meeting in London, a great crowd had gathered to hear Campbell speak. At the beginning of the meeting, while sitting on the rostrum, God spoke to his heart. He leaned over to the man who was to introduce him and said, "I must leave." The man said, "Sir, are you ill?" He said, "No, I must go to the Hebrides." The man protested, "But

Brother Campbell, these have come to hear you speak." He said, "I must go."

Upon arising, he signaled to a young couple who was traveling with him. Their name was Waters. He instructed them to go pack and make preparations to go to the Hebrides. In obedience, they did what he asked and found themselves in transit, without knowledge of what would transpire when they arrived. Much has been written of the events. History recorded that there was a power that swept upon city after city, and every light at night would suddenly come on at the same time. The cries were heard by people weeping and begging God to save them.

It is also indicated that in one particular city the revival had not yet come. A group of people were there praying in a home. Suddenly, in tears, a man cried out to God in complete brokenness, giving over all that he was to the Lord and begging Him to do in that city what was done in the others. Of the many wondrous events that happened, it could only be described as a revival, visitation from Almighty God. This, as always, is the result of brokenness and praying as promised in **II Chronicles 7:14**. As always in the course of every great move of God you will find God raising up those who can intercede in faith. Such was a young man of 17 years by the name of Donald Smith. In his area of Arnol, the church was in dead formalism. A prayer meeting was called to plead the promises of God. Just after midnight, young Donald Smith stood and prayed this prayer as related by Owen Murphy.

"Lord, You made a promise, are You going to fulfill it? We believe that You are a convenant keeping God. Will You be true to Your covenant? You have said that You will pour water upon him that is thirsty and floods upon the dry ground. Lord, I know not how these ministers stand in Your Presence, but if I know my own heart I know where I stand, and I tell Thee now that I am thirsty. Oh, I am thirsty for a manifestation of the Presence and Power of God!. And Lord, before I sit down, I want to tell You that Your honour is at stake!"

Immediately, the house, as in an earthquake, began to rattle and shake. At that instant, lights began to flash on all through that hamlet. It is recorded that people fell out of their beds and upon their knees, begging God for salvation. It was an instantaneous, glorious, sweeping movement of God's Spirit and Power across the area.

In Berneray things were very difficult as the stream of religious life was very low; churches were empty and prayer meetings were practically non-existent. In view of this, a wire was sent to the praying men of Barvas to come and assist in prayer, and bring them Donald Smith, the 17-year old boy to whom God had imparted the amazing ministry of prayer. Halfway through his message, the preacher stopped, and called out: "DONALD WILL YOU LEAD US IN PRAYER?" Standing to his feet, he began to pour out his heart before God in agonizing intercession for the people of the island, and reminding God that He was the great "covenant-keeping God." Suddenly, it seemed as though the heavens were rent and God swept into the church. People everywhere were stricken by the Power of God, as the Spirit swept through in great convicting power. Outside, startling things were taking place. *Simultaneously the Spirit of God had swept over the homes and area around the village, and everywhere people came under great conviction of sin. Fishermen out in their boats, men behind their looms, men at the pit bank, a merchant out with his truck, school teachers examining their papers, were gripped by God and by 10 o'clock the roads were black with people, streaming from every direction to the church.* As the preacher came out of the church, the Spirit of God swept in among the people on the road as wind. They gripped each other in fear. In agony of soul they trembled; many wept, and some fell to the ground in great conviction of sin. Three men were found lying by the side of the road, in such distress of soul that they could not even speak - *yet they had never been to church!*

It must be noted here that Campbell came only to stay a few days, but the Spirit of God kept him there for over two years. He could not leave. History has proven that in all of the phenomenal happenings of that period of time, the Glory of God came in answer to prayers of brokenness. Beloved, it worked then. It will work now. There must, however, be a yielded "intercessor," (*Isaiah 59:16*).

In this event, as well as all other moves of God, you will begin hearing or reading of the miracles that were performed by God's Power. And, in every case, you can trace the great circumstances of those revivals back to their origins. You will always find that they had their births with one or more individuals in prayer, totally broken before God. Through intercession, under the weight of the sin of that nation, city, church, or a burden for another individual, God fell in Power. Someone, somewhere, will have always paid the price. God gets into the matter by one of two ways, either by prayer or judgment.

The Hebrides revival is history and not fiction. It is a real event. It really happened. No man can say it was mass psychology or hypnosis. How can one explain the instantaneous coming of the Lord in such power that an entire city would be thrust upon its knees at the same time, crying out to God? Drunkards fell as dead men upon the streets, then stood up cleansed, delivered, liberated, set free, born again by the Power of God. Such was the glorious presence of God in answer to prayer. And it could happen again. It must happen again.

Please, God, break us and make it so.

"Charles Cowman, a missionary in the Far East, learned the same formula for an abiding work. Let us hear what he says:

'If any will dare to venture forth on a path of separation, putting himself from a future aid and from all self-originated effort; content to walk with God alone, with no help from any but Him -- such will find that all resources of the Divine Almightiness will be placed at his disposal, and that the resources of Omnipotence must be exhausted before His cause fail for want of help.'"

It is impossible to explain how the Power of God has been birthed into the hearts of the people in the Methodist Church. History records in the early Korean revival that God's Power was so strong that multitudes were swept into God's Kingdom. This will happen again by the power of prayer, if we pray humbled or broken.

One of my favorite studies is the Welsh revival. Here, God exploded across the lives of hardened miners, taking their hearts and melting them through the preaching of an 18-year old young man so anointed and so committed to a sovereign God that men trembled because of their sins. It is interesting to note that the theme of that move of God was the statement declared from the lips of a broken people: "Lord, bend us, break us. Lord, bend us, break us." That kind of declaration, coupled with a desire within the individual, will invoke God's Power on every occasion. Oh, the wondrous joy that it brings!

It is said:

"Whatever you and I may be privileged to do for

Him, let it be too Scriptural in its character and too decided in its results to be mistaken for the works of men."

Anonymous

Until we are broken before God, all of our efforts will be fleshly. All of our activities will be physical labor as we strive to build the church rather than the Kingdom. When people begin to pray and see others as Christ sees them, saved or lost, religion will be discovered as a barrier rather than blessing. From there, people will begin to be broken over their sins and we will again see these victories. It can happen. IT MUST HAPPEN! God make it so.

For about ten years, we had the privilege of going to Switzerland several times a year. We stayed in a city called Chateau d-Oex. The reason for our constant return there was not only to minister to the local community in which we had made many friends, but to also study and pray in the place where James Stewart had come to write his many books on the revival in Europe. This man witnessed the Power of God as result of broken praying. For a season, the fires of God burned in the hearts of men in that part of the world. As we visited time and again with the owners of this Christian establishment, Brother and Sister Owens would share with us what they actually saw, heard, and felt of the Grace of God as people in Canada and Europe wept before the Lord. Our hearts, at that time, were introduced to the reality that a great move could happen again in this period in history, if the same conditions were met.

During our stays there, we saw on several occasions a miraculous touch of God. I personally believe that revival is atmospheric. When God visited His people, there was a presence of power beyond any expression. It then "spilled" from the place where it first fell, into the surrounding areas. Like rain, beginning with mercy drops, came the showers of blessing. How much we learned of God in that wonderful place of prayer in Switzerland!

History has also recorded the move of God in Argentina in the 1950's and '60s. People were broken before the Lord and were swept into the Kingdom of God by the power of prayer. An old saint of God who has now gone on to be with the Lord, and who taught in the area of revival, made this statement: "Oh, God, do it again. Do it again." Could we say that?

My beloved, I know we can see this in our time. It can and must happen again. Never before has it become so vital that God's Spirit begin to move upon the hearts of men and women. A curtain is coming down in this period of history on all that we know. The stage is rapidly being set for all end-time things declared in the Old and New Testaments. There is a falling away. Men's hearts are failing. Things are waxing worse and worse, and evil is accelerating on a daily basis. Peace is the cry but there is no peace. Yet the Scripture promises, *"where sin did abound, grace did much more abound."* If Christians would pray to be broken, God would visit us in the midst of these "signs of the times." History is about over. We must now stand, having our *"loins girded about with truth."* We must *"stand fast therefore in the liberty wherewith Christ has made us free, and be not entangled with the yoke of bondage."*

The battle field that we're entering now, more so than in any period in recent history, is prayer. Drastic times call for drastic Biblical measures. God's Power operates only by the Holy Spirit, not by procedures. His Glory comes only to a broken, contrite, spirit: one who trembles at His Word and who knows that there is nothing good in himself; one who, through the light of co-identification of His Presence in Spirit, has seen the darkness of his own being; and one who has cried from a position of loneliness in self that God's Power would come to his life. He pleads as Job and Isaiah, *"I must have you, Lord. I must have you. I beseech you to take over my life. Here I am, send me."*

For this ever to happen again, there must be a breaking of what we are. We must be exposed to ourselves, that we may see in that glorious presence of convicting Light that we are wretched and completely absent of any personal ability to do anything of God. Then we will cry in desperation, *"Father, forgive me of my sin and fill me with Your Spirit. Take complete control of my life."* It is only when we get totally honest and become transparent that revival will come and God's Power will flow. And it will begin with one.

George Bowen wrote:

"It matters little what you have, so long as you have God; it matters little where you have been, so long as you have been to Calvary; it matters little whom you know, as long as you know God; it matters little what you possess, as long as you are possessed of the Holy Ghost.

God has been known to use a stick in the hand of Moses, a stone in the sling of David, and a staff in the hand of Benaiah. He used vermin to move Pharaoh, an ass to move Balaam, and a fish to move Jonah. His equipment is inexhaustible, and his methods of labor innumerable. All He needs is a yielded instrument."

Over the years, the door of brokenness has led me to real revival. I have learned that it comes only when God's Spirit falls upon the hearts of men, causing them to see themselves as they really are. That revelation will bring weeping under conviction. It is my personal belief that the hallmark of revival is open confession. I have never experienced it any other way. When the Holy Spirit comes upon a congregation, suddenly they begin to confess their sins openly. In a recent conference on brokenness, a man raised his hand and asked me this question: "Brother Bonner, why is it that in the last several days of this meeting, I have suddenly remembered that when I was five years of age I was molested?"

With tears streaming down his cheeks, he was so desperately concerned why the memories had suddenly flooded back as he had begun to pray to be broken. I said, "Beloved, that spirit is hidden within you to destroy you. As you have begun in this meeting to pray that God would take over your life, He has uncovered the darkness of your soul and its baggage. The Greek term for demon spirits is 'persons without bodies.' They inhabit humans to control and destroy them. However, through true broken confession, the ground is retaken, and its binding powers are destroyed." We then led this man in open confession to forgive the individual who had molested him and to attack that spiritual stronghold by declaring, "Father, in the Name of Jesus Christ, I forgive the person who harmed me." Then we had him pray, "I praise You that this happened to me." In doing so, God was made sufficient in the matter, and His Grace overwhelmed the damage and drove out the demonic bondage. As he prayed before the congregation in agreement with us, (*Matthew 18:19*), this young father was liberated. The joy of his confession was that it began real revival in that service, which always happens when God's Spirit falls upon people. Another person began to cry aloud. Without shame, and through tears of brokenness, she expressed the occurrence of the same kind of event in her early life. Again, through prayer and confession, it was broken. Before the meeting was over, God swept through that assembly as revival fell. The pastor later said that in all his years of pastoring, he had only experienced that move of God one other time. That church is going on with God! Those who confessed openly burst out of spiritual darkness through brokenness, and entered into God's Glorious Light.

Always remember that Satan works in the hidden areas of your past. God works in the openness of your present and future. Until we are transparent with our lives, openly confessing, the devil will always have avenues to destroy. You must be self-exposed to hear from God. You must be honest with your life. The strongholds within you must be revealed to you. You, in turn, must respond by confessing them, (*James 5:16*).

SWEET MEMORIES

Beloved, people must see Christ in us. That which must be seen is not the message of our mouth or the activity of our religion, but the manifestation of His Glory through our lives. When we're totally transparent and obedient to God, the marvelous experience of the transformed life begins to come through us.

The Bible says, in *John 4:23-24*:

"But the hour cometh and now is when the true worshippers shall worship the Father in spirit and in truth; for the Father seeketh such to worship Him. God is a Spirit; and they that worship Him must worship Him in spirit and in truth."

When you were born from above in salvation, drawn into the kingdom by the Spirit of God, the Holy Spirit came to dwell within you, (*John 6:44*). That Spirit is locked inside with the one desire to be the guiding, transforming force of your life. The believer, as the Scripture states, is a three person entity. In layman's terms, a "trichotomy." He is "body, soul, and spirit." The body is the outer covering. The soul is the personality. The spirit is what is given from heaven that has with it the knowledge that God is, (*Romans 1:20*). Now, when the individual is born again, the Holy Spirit is capsulated within the spirit of man. God commands him then to be "*led of the spirit.*" So, for the brilliancy of the Light to shine through and illuminate, cleansing of the outer vessel must occur. The choice of whom one will serve is decided by the soul or personality of the individual.

During the early days of my childhood, my mother would send me to spend two weeks in the summer with an aunt and uncle who had a farm in a small town called Cuero, Texas. Some of the greatest memories I have of those pre-teen years are of riding a two-car train called a "dinky." The trip was a one-hundred fifty mile journey. After about six hours, we would begin to pass the farms that belonged to members of my mother's family. Upon arrival, my uncle would pick me up at the train station in Cuero, and we would journey down the highway that followed those same tracks. I would get to sit in the back of the pickup with a cousin. For this city-raised boy under 12, it was the adventure of my life. Wonderful remembrances!

I spent those memorable nights in that farmhouse, listening to the turkeys as they roosted in the trees for the evening, and enjoying the sounds of the wind playing its melody through a screened-in back porch where we slept. The roof was made of tin, and on those splendid evenings when it rained, the cool wind would blow and the sounds that the rain would make upon the metal house top would bring sleep to its deepest, most peaceful point.

The meals were taken at a handmade supper table that had a bench against the wall and chairs around the sides. I sat on the bench. There were wonderful foods, consisting of bacon from the smokehouse, bread cooked in a wood oven which we ate with homemade catsup and, one of my favorite things, hot corn bread crumbled in cold milk and eaten with great gusto! How precious those days! As the song says, "Ah, sweet memories."

One night while staying in that home, I saw something that would indelibly remain in my mind for my entire lifetime. God planted this as a seed in my heart, knowing that someday I would speak His Word. As I recall, we were sitting in the living room, having come in from the front porch because of the mosquitoes. I was trying to look at a magazine. The light was not very strong, and so I did what I had seen others in that family do. Lighting at night was provided by kerosene oil lamps with glass chimneys. I was not very familiar with it, but I assumed that to get more light, you took the little round knob on the side and turned up the wick. I did this and went back to my magazine and was still unable to see clearly. I applied more twisting to that knob and soon great billows of black smoke were coming out of the top of the chimney.

My aunt walked in and saw what was going on. She blew out the lamp. I had assumed by this action that she was saying it was time to go to bed as there was wonderful, loving authority in that household. However, as I got up, she stated, "Wait just a moment." Soon, the chimney of that oil lamp cooled. She removed it from its metal prongs, took her chicken feed sack dish towel and pushed it inside the glass. Then she began to turn the cloth and finally pulled it through. She turned the wick down to where it was barely showing, at which time she took a kitchen match, always present in the box on the table, and struck it. Applying it to the wick, a very small yellow flame was to emit. Ah, but then a miracle was performed. When she pulled the chimney back down over those little metal prongs, suddenly that small yellow flame exploded into a bright blue light that captured the darkness of that room with illumination. I was fascinated by the event. I looked at my book and all the details were there as that light revealed its etchings.

Some years later, in the study of the Word of God, I ran across verses that sparked this event back to my memory. Within us, is the Holy Spirit, if we have truly been born again. God's promise is that He is literally a *"lamp to our feet and a light to our path."* That inward Light is the illuminating factor to all that we do if we're led by and walk in the Spirit.

The Amplified Bible says in *Ephesians 2:10*, *"We are to take the paths which He prepared ahead of time."* Most of us stumble through life, falling into one hole and then crawling out of it, only to stumble again while walking in prayerless darkness to another hole. I remind you of *Psalm 35:7* that says, *"They have digged a pit for my soul."* Yet, through these breakings comes inner cleansing as we get serious with God. Then one day, we desire and begin to search for the transformed life. It is at that point we learn that God becomes sufficient with His Grace in the midst of the crisis. We stand in awe, bathed in the Glory of His Being, and fall in love with His Life in us and through us.

There is a verse of scripture, in *Philippians 3:3*, that in the Greek translations says, *"We worship Him in the Spirit and by the Spirit."* It means that there will be no true worship except from the position of what God does through us. All the rest that is done is the activity of religion, with an occasional touch of grace that comes in moments of tribulation, as we throw ourselves on Him, crying for mercy. He must, by our choosing, become the desire of our hearts in all matters from that point in time, (*Romans 12:1-2*). However, this will never come in the life of any individual until he is broken before God. In that transparent state of confession, the light begins to shine through. How tragic it is to fall in hole after hole when all the time there is within us the light that would "*guide us into all truth*," if we would seek openly to be broken, honest, and cleansed before the Lord!

II Corinthians 3:18 in the Amplified states:

"*And all of us as with unveiled face, [because we] continued to behold [in the Word of God] as in a mirror the glories of the Lord are constantly being transfigured into His very own image, in ever-increasing splendor and from one degree of glory to another; [for this comes] from the Lord [who is] the Spirit.*"

My beloved, as we begin to be broken before God, our eyes are opened. While we behold the Truth of the Word, it becomes Life and Breath and Being, instead of paper and ink and cover. Through the Scripture, we see in a mirror the Glory of the Lord. When that happens through brokenness, we become transfigured into His Image and changed by His Power as we live and experience "*from glory to glory,*" (*II Corinthians 3:18*). These are not downward steps. They progress upward toward the heavenlies, into "*His Kingdom come, His Will to be done.*" God says that it is in ever-increasing splendor, from one degree to another, and it comes to us from the Lord who is the Spirit. In that contrite state before God, the Lord works within us and through us and we become more and more like Him. Please understand, there is no true ministry except His extension of His Life by way of His children. Anything done in the flesh is experienced in the name of religion, not by the Power of God. We must be humbled and broken.

The Scripture states, "*Behold, his soul which is lifted up is not upright in him; [but the just shall live by his faith]*", (*Hebrews 2:4*).

Andrew Murray wrote:

"The great test of whether the holiness we profess to seek or to attain is truth and life, will be whether it be manifest in the increasing humility it produces. In the creature, humility is the one thing needed to allow God's holiness to dwell in him and shine through him. In Jesus, the Holy One of God who makes us holy, a divine humility was the secret of His Life and His Death and His exaltation; the one infallible test of our holiness will be the humility before God and man which marks us. Humility is the bloom and beauty of holiness.

The chief mark of counterfeit holiness is the lack of humility. Every seeker after holiness needs to be on his guard, lest unconsciously what was begun in the spirit is perfected in the flesh, and pride creep in where its presence is least expected."

FORGIVE AND FORGET

Finally, we must make reconciliation. In fact, it is imperative for true worship. God commands that if anyone has ever harmed, persecuted, or despitefully used you, then it must be forgiven. He tells us in **Matthew 6:14-15** (**Amplified**), that if someone has trespassed against you in a reckless or willful way, you must leave that sin of unforgiveness. You must let it go. You have to give up resentment. In so doing, your Heavenly Father will forgive you. For if you do not forgive others their trespasses, or those things done recklessly or willfully, and if you do not give up resentment, neither will your Father forgive you your trespasses.

So much is said in the Scripture about the sin of unforgiveness. **Psalm 66:18** states that, "**Iniquity will hide His face from you.**" He makes the same kind of declaration in **Isaiah 59:2**. So, if you're trying to worship and move to a true place of victory by the Power of God but you're rebelling at forgiving, God will not minister to and through your life. Remember when Job was broken and he was taken into the test to pray for his friends, he did not resist or reject it based on their attitude toward him. He literally, with a broken heart, overwhelmed in love for God, prayed and God forgave their trespasses.

You must be reconciled. God commands it in **Matthew 5:23-24** when He states:

> "**Therefore, if thou bring thy gift to the altar and there rememberest that thy brother hath ought against thee; leave there thy gift before the altar, and go thy way; first be reconciled to thy brother, and then come offer thy gift.**"

It is imperative that you forgive.

Incidentally, when you pray to be broken, God will reveal to you all that Satan has done to sow into the soil of your personality the rotten seeds and resentments of your past. You must confess them and forgive. Then you will see each man as God sees him, and will know that the bitterness you've experienced has been authored by Satan to drive you away from hearing from God and operating in the Spirit. You must be reconciled in order to worship, so says *Colossians 3:13*. It is also stated in *Ephesians 4:32*:

> *"For you must be kind one to another and tenderhearted, forgiving one another, even as God, for Christ's sake, hath forgiven you."*

In the case of the Power of God falling upon those in the upper room at Pentecost, it is my personal belief that the ten days there were spent not only in prayer, but in open confession of sin as the Holy Spirit prepared them for His coming. In *Acts 1:14*, the Scripture teaches that they *"All continued with one accord in prayer and supplication."* The word "continued" is from the Greek term "proskartere," which means "to persevere and stand firmly in one mind." I believe they were broken, as perhaps no other group in history, as they wept and begged for the return of Christ in His Spirit as He promised.

Then, God's Holy Spirit entered into this place of time through the door of brokenness and tears, and through the confession of sin to each other, (*James 5:16*). We are told in *Acts 2:1*:

> *"That when the day of Pentecost was fully come, they were all with one accord in one place."*

This means they were united in faith and prayer with one burning desire. Then *verse 2* shares that:

> *"Suddenly there came a sound from Heaven as*

*a rushing mighty wind and it filled the house
where they were sitting. Cloven tongues of fire
sat on each of them and they were all filled
with the Holy Ghost."*

In and by this Power, they began to be spoken through by
the Spirit of God, proclaiming Jesus the Messiah. When the
Holy Spirit comes upon an individual, Jesus is always shown to
and through the person as God Incarnate. Today continues the
Ministry of the Holy Spirit through our lives. In the light of
what is promised in *II Chronicles 7:14*, God's Spirit will come
in mighty power if we are broken.

For us, it all begins in our obedience to meet and wait,
such as we are commanded to do in *Joel, chapters one and
two*: to call a solemn assembly, then in brokenness and
desperation pray and tarry until He comes in Power. The result
of waiting is the Holy Spirit revealing us to ourselves as we are.
When we are broken, He begins to cleanse us through our
confession until the Light of Christ breaks through our lives and
we become open and transparent. From that position, people
can see all the way to the Person of Christ who lives within.
The chorus of the old hymn by B. B. McKinney, says

> "Let others see Jesus in you.
> Let others see Jesus in you.
> Keep telling the story,
> Be faithful and true.
> Let others see Jesus in you."

Transparency is the door to righteousness. To move to
that place means to openly confess your sins one to another and
to pray one for another so that you personally may be healed
from deep bondage. To reach this place, you must forgive. You
must attack every negative memory with praise until you can

talk about it without becoming emotional. When you have become openly honest and transparent, God's Spirit will come alive in you, according to His Will. Forgive and you will forget. It is by this that the Power of God, through the Blood of His Son, will cleanse you from all unrighteousness. In this event, God says, "***Then will I hear from heaven and heal their land ...***"

The man, Jonathan Edwards, was just that: a man. But he was totally yielded to God and was used mightily. Charles Finney, renowned for the Glory of God on his life, was just a man, broken and filled with God. Evan Roberts was just 18-years old when he yielded all to his Heavenly Father, and Wales was shaken to its core. Who could forget the Wesleys, Charles Spurgeon, Duncan Campbell, Corrie Ten Boom, Manley Beasley, and on and on? All broken. All committed. And all transformed. Each of those named, however, would be the first to say, "It is just God. I had nothing to do with what had happened or what was going on."

Would you be willing to ask Him to do it through you? "***Ask and it shall be given, seek and ye shall find.***"

Andrew Murray wrote:

"We want to get possession of the power and use it; God wants the power to get possession of us and use us. If we give ourselves to the Power to rule in us, the Power will give itself to us to rule through us."

Pray, "God, do it again. Please break me that You can get it done through me. I beg you. Here I am, send me."

CHAPTER SIX

THE NATURE OF THE BEAST

It has been said that brokenness will lead you to humility, or humility before the Lord will lead you to brokenness. There are two paths to the Cross in this event. For those of us who are hardheaded and yet seek to be used of God, we go through great tribulation of soul. Through one event of shaking after another, the ministry of the Holy Spirit is created within us. As I have stated earlier, I have, over the years, had a growing desire to be totally committed to God. It seems, however, that when I reached the right condition to be used, pride would again come as our name would be projected as the reason for the good results in crusades and meetings. God would then back away from my spirit. I would find desolation and darkness as I pulled at the web of Satan's trap of conceit. Finally, I would once more gain freedom and victory in my walk with the Lord. How soon I forget!

James 4:10 says, *"Humble yourselves in the sight of the Lord, and He shall lift you up."* Regarding this, P. T. Forsyth wrote:

> "Humility is a great mystery to itself. It is the amazement of the redeemed soul before itself, or rather before Christ in itself. It may take the shape of modesty before men, or it may not; humility is not anything which we have in the sight or thought of other men at all. It is the soul's attitude before God."

> "... It can take very active, assertive, and even fiery

shape in dealing with men. It is not timidity or nervousness. It is not shy, not embarrassed, not hesitant, not self-conscious, not ill-at-ease, not a seeker of back seats or mien of low shoulders and drooping head. Yet it is not self-sufficient in a proud and stoic reserve, nor self-assertive in a public Pharisee fashion. It can never be had either by imitating the humble or by mortifying the flesh. Devotion is not humility, though humility is devout. It is only to be had by the mastery of the Cross which taketh away the self-rapt guilt of the world."

There are some who are so yielded to Christ and are so humbled in His Presence that they work in His Grace and find that glorious walk in the Spirit. Growing in humility has with me brought times of begging the Lord for restoration during those dark hours of separation from His Wonderful Glory. *"Oh wretched man that I am"*. It is, in essence, the cycle of the Christian life.

Amidst seasons of *"tribulation that worketh patience"* is the light within us that reflects to us our true soulish natures, revealing to us what we really are. Shame grips our hearts because of the "show" or false "spiritual maturity" that we have displayed, thereby taking the glory from the Lord. This is the "nature of the beast." Satan moves on our emotions to control our flesh, until we are overcome by the position of pride, lust, or fear. As a result, we lose spiritual consciousness of the power that is within us in the person of the Holy Spirit.

When you squeeze a lemon, you get what is in it. That's why God allows tribulation within us, according to *James 1*. Under those circumstances, we truly see ourselves. In today's environment, there is an endeavor to place before people a "cool" or "self-reliant" image, when inside there is really devastation of personality. It is interesting to note the explosion of psychiatry and Christian clinical psychologists in today's world. They work from both sides: one through Freudian science, and the other through Biblical presentation of truths that can be applied as "principles" for the person to overcome the problems of the demonic world system.

But you must understand the position of principles. It is the packaging of so-called biblical truths to be studied, counseled, and applied by an individual to his emotions in order to regain control of his life and being. Principles, however, are still the activities of Christians doing Christian activity based on the concepts of man in the light of his particular doctrine. With over 20,000 denominations and many writers composing from the descriptive posture of their own faith and belief, we are finding materials that are not windows to a lighted path, but reasoning through emotion and psyche.

I know the Scripture teaches that we must *"reason together."* Thus it is always Biblical and good in therapy to be in open discussion and acknowledgment of the strongholds of the life. That is the power of *James 5:16* in the confession of faults one to another. In fact, all psychiatry and psychology, Biblical, Freudian, or otherwise, could be wrapped up in that verse. It states:

> *"Confess your faults one to another, and pray one for another, that ye may be healed. The effectual fervent prayer of a righteous man availeth much."*

It is so designed by God in the individual that when a person finally exposes the deepest areas of his life that have caused fear, roots of bitterness, or rejection of memory within them, then the exposure to light by open confession brings healing within. Satan operates in the past, Christ operates in the present, as well as in the future. The key to it all is to be open and transparent. This destroys the power of the enemy to accuse, (*Revelation 12:10*).

Again, principles are the blending of human personality with the Word, or Scripture, based on the Light a person has received within the dogma of his denomination. It is an attempt to work out his problems using Scripture. When a person is broken before God and seeks a continual walk at that level, the roots of bitterness and unforgiveness will surface from the memory of his innermost being. When that happens, the waters begin to clear of impurities, and victory is experienced.

MUDDY WATER

Some years ago we were in a conference where the speaker held up a clear glass before the audience. To illustrate the sin-life of people, he filled it with dirt. He then described that dirt as being our unregenerate form without Christ. Then he said: "Here's what happens when a person is born again and the Holy Spirit comes to live within him. He begins to seek the Lord and practice the Presence of the Lord daily through prayer."

He placed that glass underneath a faucet and turned the water so that the stream would hit directly on top of the soil. Needless to say, it was a sight as mire and silt not only splashed, but ran over the outside of the glass. It made one think for a moment about what God sees on the inside as He begins to cleanse us through the daily washing of the Water of the Word, filling us with the Spirit, (*Ephesians 5:18*).

It seemed to me that the demonstration was over and the

point was made. However, there was more as he said, "Wait a minute." The water was coming down in a stream, still hitting the dirt. The glass was totally visible as muddy liquid ran over the side, and small streams of sludge moved away from the vessel. As we were waiting for his point, he stated, "Just a second more." Then he said, "You're about to see a phenomenon. Watch the darkest part of the glass."

I could see the water purging the dirt, with the mud cascading over the outside. But then I began to notice what he was saying. The dirt itself, in the darkest area of the glass, was receding as the constant flow of clean liquid went into it. After a few moments, the stream itself and the strength of its flow reached the bottom of that vessel. Still, it was muddy. Still, it was dirty. Yet the glass was very evident in its presence.

But then, as the water swirled, and mud was coming over the top, I began to notice the bottom of the glass. At first it was dirty, then milky, then basically cloudy. Suddenly, it became clear at the bottom as the silt made its way to the top. Then an amazing thing happened! The glass totally disappeared. All you could see was the water cascading over the outside of it. Salvation and cleansing, God's Way!

Beloved, such is the life of the believer who is in constant pursuit of the Lord Jesus Christ, and the filling and working of the Holy Spirit. We are still subject to sin, and will be, for there is none totally righteous; *"no not one."* As we grow in grace for a season, there is so much that is vile and unclean that continues to come out. In the process of maturing in Him, there is the cloudy time and the cleansing time. The pursuing of a daily relationship with Christ becomes so overwhelming to the satanic and demonic strongholds which remain inside, a change within begins. As we remain in the continual commitment to the Father in prayer, there is the constant flowing in of the cleansing water; in this case the Holy Spirit, (*John 4:14*). When we're filled through brokenness with the Holy Spirit, the inner vessel is cleansed, and God's Glory covers us, (**"But, be ye being filled," Ephesians 5:18**). Then, we walk in the Spirit. We are alive in the Spirit. We are filled with the Spirit. We operate in the ministry and flow of the Spirit, (**Galatians 5:22-24**). We are covered and running over, as long as we stay under the water.

You say, "Brother Bonner, what do I get out of that?" The greatest joy you will ever know. You see, when you are broken before the Lord, released within you is the Power of God and the Holy Spirit. The inner man then covers the outer man and you have His Ministry over and through your life. You then become **"led of the Spirit."** From that position, you **"walk in the Light,"** for your light is no longer hidden **"under a bushel,"** but in this case, is on a candlestick as a **"lamp unto my feet and a light unto my path."**

Another way to look at this is to understand the fact that you are a trichotomy: body, soul, and spirit. The body is the outer shell. The soul is your personality, mind, emotions, and will. The spirit is placed in you by God. When you become saved or born again, the Holy Spirit moves within the spirit of your inner man. The body is still the outer shell. Your soul, (you in your personality,) is the one who chooses the business of the flesh or the control of the Spirit.

STANDING RIGHT WHERE GOD IS

The soul of the carnal Christian, (one who operates by feelings rather than by faith,) says "yes" to the body: whatever it wants to do, wherever it wants to go, whatever it would like to eat. The soul submits totally to the pleasures of the flesh.

Consequently, the flesh of that Christian is operated by demons. But there is no such thing as a demon-possessed, born again, Child of God. The Holy Spirit and the unholy spirit cannot dwell in the same spirit of man.

Therefore, these evil spirits negotiate with the soul on what is the pleasure of the flesh by bringing before the individual things that would please the body. It is the word *"wiles"* of *Ephesians 6:11*. Satan knows exactly what to do to destroy your walk with God. Sometimes, he creates circumstances that attack pride through the door of insecurity. Often he devises to consume through lust. He desecrates a wonderful gift given by God to the body, to capture within its realm love for an individual who has chosen to be a lifetime spouse.

Again, I'm talking about the desires within marriage that are a natural gift from God for two who have chosen, first of all, to walk in the Spirit, submitting first to the Lord and then to each other, (*Ephesians 5:21*). However, there is a consuming of lust that encompasses many areas. This is satanically and demonically activated to destroy the life of the Christian. This is found in *Galatians 5:16*: *"This I say then, walk in the Spirit and you shall not fulfill the lust of the flesh."*

In the light of this and the movement of demons upon human flesh, *I John 2:16* states:

"For all that is in the world, the lust of the flesh, the lust of the eyes, and the pride of life, is not of the Father, but is of the world."

In the unbroken individual, there is orchestrated for his eyes and ears every enticing activity to destroy. In the present day demise of true Christianity, prayer time has been taken over by television, and divine order has lost place to confusion within the household, as the sounds of many voices direct the life-styles of those involved.

One enticing destruction of the flesh through lust is described as the desire for material things. People are so demonically seduced that they purchase on credit beyond their abilities, soon facing accusations in their own lives. They are unable to keep up with their payments. From this posture they are depressed and broken and are left without faith.

The lust of the eyes is the place of covetousness that has a craving for more and more until it overcomes all reason, and wants to become central instead of waiting upon the Lord to provide. Then, the pride of life is the enemy's strongest door, to bring in confusion while we try to "keep up" with other individuals, either by design or desire.

Yet the broken vessel drains the carnal life of the normal, fleshly Christian. As the dirt pours out from the inflow of the fresh water of the Spirit, the Light of God shines through the breaks. By His Power, suddenly the path becomes lighted. By the light of the lamp unto our feet, we walk around the pits that have been dug for our soul, (*Psalm 35:7*).

My beloved friend, please understand. There will be no rule and reign of the Holy Spirit in your life until the outer man is broken before the Lord.

God says:

"For Christ also hath once suffered for sins, the just for the unjust, that He might bring us to God, being put to death in the flesh, but quickened by the Spirit," (I Peter 3:18).

As Christ died upon the cross, He took our sins in His Body on the tree, that He might be our bridge to God. The vessel for this redemptive package, however, was being put to death in the flesh, only to be quickened by the Spirit, so that in the process He would arise from the grave.

Such is our life through co-crucifixion with Christ. As we are crucified daily by choice through prayer, (*Galatians 2:20*), so are we quickened by the Holy Spirit in resurrected life through faith. In the progression of that relationship, the Spirit of God shines through us, and our ministry begins to be His. Please understand. It is only through that kind of life that God gets anything done through us. For it is the resurrected life that brings the righteousness of God into the right standing with man. Righteousness means, "right standing with God," or standing right where God is in you.

> "The door of faith," said Alexander MacLaren, "is a narrow one; for it lets no self-righteousness, no worldly glories, no dignities through. We are kept outside till we strip ourselves of crowns and royal robes, and stand clothed only in the hair shirt of penitence. We must make ourselves small to get in. We must creep on our knees, so low is the vault; we must leave everything outside, so narrow is it. We must go in one by one. The door opens into a palace, but it is too straight for anyone who trusts to himself."

When you are broken and your desire is completely yielded to His, then He ministers His Will through you. From that posture comes the dynamics of joy beyond any description. Love, as the Person of Christ in you, overwhelms beyond anything ever experienced. With it also comes the peace that passes all understanding, that even in the face of death, there is grace, complete with joy to get to the other side. How great our God and how wonderful His attributes in giving to us first the privilege of ministering His Life and then His rewards here and after!

The truth is, we must understand that there is a call to brokenness in order to develop the consciousness of God's Glory through our lives. Without breaking, we can never know the true presence of His Glory and the purpose of the Holy Spirit. There are many seasons in developing righteousness in the life of the individual. There are times of winter, when the cold winds of doubt, fear, and accusation by the enemy, the heart of the person, driving him desperately, by prayer and praise, to the Will of God.

These events give birth to springtime, in all of its glory! The trees of our lives begin to bear fruit as we are attached to the vine. As a result, the countenance of joy blossoms! Soon to follow is the heat of summer, and finally autumn, when the leaves begin to shed from the limbs after the fruit has been taken. Back again we are led, into the cycle of winter and drawing-in of life for a season of new brokenness to bring new and higher growth. This is the cycle of development in the Christian as he experiences living "from glory to glory." As a dear friend of mine once said in a message, which literally expressed my experience in the Christian life, "If you're not in trouble, it is because you have just gotten out, and you're about to go back in." It is the cycle of the spiritual life that develops the character of Christ and a relationship with God's Spirit, whereby He becomes not only the ministry through us, but sufficient in all matters. In that procedure, however, is a spiral that is always ascending. For every circuit of breaking is a step to a higher experience with the Lord. Through it, in growth, you become more praiseworthy of the negative events that are happening to you. Plus, you learn a new dimension of faith you have never experienced before. God, in past breaking, had become sufficient in the matter. Therefore, after the first moments that fear grips your heart, you again remember that in everything, God's place and purpose is there, for **"all things do work together,"** (*II Corinthians 12:9*).

Charles Spurgeon stated:

"It seems Jehovah's way is to lower those whom He means to raise and to strip those whom He intends to clothe. If it is His way, it is the wisest and best way."

Always remember that you are only as mature as the level of your praise in the midst of your tribulation. *Ephesians 5:20* teaches us, *"Giving thanks always for all things unto God and the Father in the Name of our Lord, Jesus Christ."* This verse is given to us in sequence, following the experience of *Ephesians 5:18*, *"Be ye (being) filled with the Holy Spirit."* It is experienced initially and then daily through prayer.

SERVANTS

For God to develop His character in the lives of Christians, He places us in situations where the circumstances involve brokenness. We finally give it all back to God. In response to our submission, we grow to an even greater dependency and to a more dynamic faith. I am reminded of some precious verses beginning in *I Peter 2:18* where the word *"servant,"* (as in household servant) is used. If we would understand the true meaning of that word, we would discover that the greatest event in life is to move from being a master to being obediently subjected to the sovereign Will of the Holy Spirit. God tells us to *"be not many masters, knowing that we shall receive the greater condemnation," (James 3:1).*

In brokenness a man becomes an extension of the hand of God through the inner working of the Holy Spirit. In this condition he continues the work of the Father here upon this earth. No man laboring for another would take over the place of authority without permission. He would make no purchase, sell no item, or involve himself in any decision that did not have the approval of the owner. So it is with the Christian life, that we, by the dynamics of His Ministry and Will, operate according to the Person of Christ in us. We must understand that all true ministry is the continuing work of the Lord Jesus Christ through our lives, at the level of our obedience. All the rest is wood, hay, and stubble, (*I Corinthians 3:12-13*).

I Peter 2:18-23 states:

"Servants, be subject to your masters in all fear; not only to the good and gentle, but also to the froward. For this is thankworthy, if a man for conscience toward God endure grief, suffering wrongfully. For what Glory is it, if, when ye be buffeted for your faults, ye shall take it patiently? But if, when ye do well, and suffer for it, ye take it patiently, this is acceptable with God. For even hereunto were ye called: because Christ also suffered for us, leaving us an example, that ye should follow in His steps: Who did no sin, neither was guile found in his mouth: Who, when he was reviled, reviled not again; when he suffered, he threatened not; but committed himself to Him that judgeth righteously."

This is the sign of yielded obedience to God's Spirit. As

servants, we are subject to our Master with all fear. In the case of our relationship with God, the word "fear" means "reverential awe" or worship. This comes because we want more than anything else to be one with God. The Holy Spirit, however, through Peter is sharing something much deeper in these scriptures. He is saying that we must have respect, not only for those who are kind and reasonable, but for those who are overbearing, and as one translation says, *"unjust and crooked."*

In order to submit, you must attack your angry, negative feelings in praise, remembering that the ministry of Satan is to divide, and the thief's desire is to kill, steal, and destroy. So, when you become discouraged in your circumstances, begin to view these situations through the "why?" of God's Will and always stay in praise for the events being experienced. Satan will set up incidents to get you to make a critical, verbal declaration regarding what is happening, and at that instant his demonic force moves into your life. Then your situation becomes worse, for the spiral or cycle at that point begins to descend rather than ascend. The Scripture says, *"it is not what goes in a person's mouth that defiles him or separates him from God, but that which comes out."* Learn to be aggressive in thanksgiving toward Satan's attacks. He is totally overcome and defeated by High Praise, (*Psalm 149:6-9*).

Now, you can know the level of your maturity based on the level of your ability to praise God in the midst of your tribulation. This, in part, is what is being said in the *19th* verse of *I Peter 2*. For if you walk with God and endure suffering because of it, God brings growth and then special honor to your life. As stated earlier, you are only as mature as your praise in the midst of your present tribulation.

Once more, you must understand that there will be

continual, joyous breaking in your life in order to bring maturity. God's purpose is to develop the character of Christ into the person of the Christian, that the ministry of the Holy Spirit can be extended through him. As the attacks come through the *"fiery darts"* being thrown, you remain in praise, for you know by past experience that in the armor of God you are totally enveloped by God's Glory and Presence. Tribulation is a wonderful thing, for in it, you get to see the astonishing hand of God working through your life. That is why God says to get excited and joyful when troubles come, (*James 1:2-4, Amplified*).

Those verses continue by telling us that we have been called to praise. People who run from tribulation and never learn to face their circumstances, (in which they would be developed into the character of Christ,) are literally desolate when conflict comes. They have no concept of direction, and no idea how to pray to seek God. They feel alone and abandoned. How tragic, and yet, in reality, it could be quite the contrary! For in our conflicts is His mighty Grace overwhelmingly sufficient. There are only two postures of prayer: one, from desperation; two, in adoration. When you can bring these two great rivers into one ocean, it becomes an unlimited reservoir and a constant source of life and victory.

Christ suffered for us, leaving us His example. Paul, in *Philippians 3:10*, declared of his own life as he cried from a wondrously filled, contrite heart, *"that I may know Him and the Power of His Resurrection and the Fellowship of His Sufferings."* It is only from that position that we come into resurrected life, which is birthed through the tomb of brokenness, raised to immortality, formed in His Glory, and developed in our lives. It is *"Christ in you, the hope of Glory."*

I Peter 2:21 (in the Amplified) states:

"For even to this were you called. It is inseparable from your vocation. For Christ also suffered for you, leaving you [His personal] example, so that you should follow on in His footsteps."

Oh, the unbounded joy of extending the life of Christ through us, to learn of Him and have the privilege of suffering unjustly, (*Matthew 5:44*)! In the process, becoming abandoned to Him, we have a complete filling of His Life in ours, resulting in a wonderful union. In everything, we stand in the midst of tribulation in praise! From the position of praise, we have the *"peace that passeth all understanding,"* even if faced with accusation. This is the true evidence of a maturing Christian life: peace in the midst of the storm.

Rising from any negative situation comes the true proving of our walk with Christ as we begin to grow up in Holy Faith, (*Jude 1:20*). Its strongest evidences are when we agree with the old hymn:

"Lord, help me live from day to day,

In such a self-forgetful way,

That even when I kneel to pray,

My prayers shall be for others,

Others, Lord, yes, others.

Let this my motto be.

Help me to live for others,

That I may live like Thee."

The mark of true obedience is a complete yielding and life of servant-hood.

THE TAIL WAGS THE DOG

To remind you again, there is no ministry except that which is done by God through you. All the rest is the activity of Christians doing Christian activities based on the concepts of man. To repeat, religion is the effort to disciple people according to one's own conclusions of what the Scripture teaches. This, for the most part, gives birth to doctrine through reasoning, rather than by revelation. In brokenness, however, there is a shaking of the individual to bring him to the experiential Truth of God.

A plea was made for position in heaven by both James and John, the sons of Zebedee. One desired to sit at the right hand of the throne, the other desired to sit at the left side when Christ came into His Glory. This is an example of how denominations start, for it is in confusion that the Spirit's Revelation to Truth ends, (*I Corinthians 14:33*). *"They have a zeal without knowledge,"* (*Romans 10:2*). Therefore, men begin to reason the rules of righteousness rather than hear within God's Will. This was true of James and John, for in knowing the nature of man, Christ had already stated to them in prior verses that these positions are not His to assign, but *"shall be given to them for whom it is prepared."*

Christ then profoundly laid out the procedures of the Christian's positional relationship with Him. He began by expressing to them what they were familiar with at that point. He explained how government worked and the rule of those who had authority and lordship over them, (*Mark 10:42-45*). Such is the kingdom of religion. Men have more desire to be subjected to popes, bishops, elders, and judges, than to prayer and brokenness before the Lord, after which the Holy Spirit might direct.

There is wisdom in counselors, and there must always be

a submission to authority. I do not negate the fact that we are to submit ourselves one to another; however, religion becomes political as structures are built, resulting in the evolution of denominations.

As we look back through the history of many denominations who were birthed through the tears of broken men and women, we find that they originally endeavored to bring into focus a profound Biblical Truth, experienced after a great move of the Spirit of God. The problem that arose is that in its perpetuation, the vision or goal of the Spirit was forgotten. Structures were/are formed to continue the movement, and self-immortalization becomes the desperate need to keep it going and growing. Then it began to die, as prior principles and tenets of their faith decayed in conviction, and worldly compromise set in as politics became the norm.

It must be remembered that every historical move of God was birthed from broken prayer and must be continued to keep God's glory in its midst. If it is forgotten, then Satan begins business as usual: religion. Incidentally, when our prayers cease to rise, Christianity crashes downwards through tradition and formalism, and eventually becomes the doctrines of demons, (*I Timothy 4:1*). Then another vision birthed in brokenness dies. As the old adage says, "The tail wags the dog."

It is the individual life broken before God that brings revival. This is what Christ said to His other disciples, who were deeply disturbed with James and John for even asking for a special place in Glory. His response to these men was:

"Whosoever will be great among you shall be your minister: And whosoever of you shall be the chiefest, shall be servant of all. For even the Son of Man came not to be ministered unto,

but to minister, and to give His life a ransom for many," (Mark 10:43-45).

What He is actually saying is that to become great ministers we must first become a servant. Please understand the use of that word as we explained it earlier. A servant is one who extends the mind and desire of his master. No one driving through the farmlands of the world, seeing laborers working in the field, and noticing there on a hill, in the distance, a home and a barn, would ever refer to the people as possessors. They would state of the owner, "Look at his crops." "Look what he is being able to raise."

Such is your relationship with Jesus Christ. God becomes your sovereign. The Holy Spirit becomes your source and force. Through brokenness you extend the ministry of Jesus Christ through your life. At that place, you serve the Lord with joyous gladness! In fact, His consistent response to this truth is that to become great, you must become small. Or, *"Whoever wishes to be most important and first in rank among you must be the slave of all," (Mark 10:44, Amplified).*

It is an evident sign of God's consuming glory in your life when you begin to live for others. The word "service" or "servant" occurs over 1,300 times in the Word of God. It is not something to strive for. It is the inevitable and wonderful result of God's consuming Spirit in the life of the individual. You become what you are in Him to the level of your abandonment to the Holy Spirit. Then, the evidence of being broken before the Lord and His consuming control of your life is that you have become a servant. A non-contrite individual will live to receive. But, the one submitted, yielded, and broken before God will live to give. In fact, you truly live at the level you give.

Charles Spurgeon wrote, "The tree grows best skyward

that grows most downward; the lower the saint grows in humility, the higher he grows in holiness."

People are being taught today how to manipulate God into their circumstances, but it will not work. This manipulation results in what we are presently seeing, and that is the death of the main-line denominations in their prayerless, powerless state. God does not yield to man. There is no ministry but His through us, and yet, in death there is still an alternative. It is resurrection. It could happen if we humbled ourselves and prayed. But only through brokenness.

Edwin Harvey tells the story of John Milne, who had offered himself as a candidate to the Missionary Society. They were sorely in need of someone to send to assist Robert Morrison, but were loathsome in sending him because of his many deficiencies. After highlighting his drawbacks, they offered him a post as a servant rather than a missionary.

John Milne replied, "If I am not judged fit to be a missionary, I will gladly go as a servant. I am willing to be a hewer of wood or a drawer of water, or to do any service that will advance the kingdom of my heavenly master."

Years afterward, Dr. Milne was recognized by all men as one of the best and most competent workers in the land. God had taken up the fragments and built them into His mission edifice in China.

Beloved, pray to be broken. The evidences will reflect your greater joy in servant-hood than in anything else you do. It's the nature of Christ through you. It is wonderful. *"He that findeth his life shall lose it; and he that loseth his life for my sake shall find it." (Matthew 10:39)* It is the key to life.

CHAPTER SEVEN

THE ADVENTURE OF ADVERSITY

Isaiah 45:7 is a unique verse. Here, God says of Himself, *"I form the light, and create darkness; I make peace, and create evil; I the Lord do all these things."* There are four major acts of God found in this Scripture. First, He forms the light. This word is the Hebrew word "owr" which means "illumination." Then, He states, *"I create darkness."* This means "the withdrawing or absence of light." Thirdly, He declares, *"I make peace,"* which means "freedom from war or civil disorders." Finally, He announces, *"I create evil."* Now, the word for "create" is "bara". It is the same word God uses in Genesis 1 to speak all into existence. *"And God said,"* (*Genesis 1:3*).

The Hebrew word for "evil" is "ra". This word is never spoken of as sin, but always of evil, or "calamity." It is also found as the word **"adversity,"** in *I Samuel 10:19*; **"grief,"** in *Nehemiah 2:10*; **"sorrow,"** in *Genesis 44:29*; **"trouble,"** in *Psalm 27:4*; **"distress,"** in *Nehemiah 2:17*; **"bad,"** in *Genesis 24:50*; **"affliction,"** in *Numbers 11:11*; **"misery,"** in *Ecclesiastics 8:6*; **"sore,"** in *Deuteronomy 6:22*; **"noisome,"** (detrimental) in *Ezekiel 14:15*; **"hurt,"** in *Genesis 26:29*; and **"wretchedness,"** in *Numbers 11:14*.

Now I have listed these to illustrate that we do reap what we sow, and that sin will bring trouble and distress to our lives. The word "ra" is translated "evil" 430 times. It is never used, however, with the concept that sin is created by God. God is the law giver, and when there is a breaking of that canon, there shall always be a reprimand by God, as we have seen by studying the events of the Old Testament, as well as the New. How we are seeing this today as the Scripture states, *"The wicked shall be turned into hell, and all the nations that forget God,"* (*Psalm 9:17*)! We are under the beginning of judgment.

With this truth in mind, we will approach brokenness from another posture. I must also say at this time that this instruction is only for the believer who wants to go on with God, and whose life is committed to righteousness. As the clouds of history darken with wars and rumors of wars, pestilence, and earthquakes in divers places, (*Matthew 24:7*), so are we, as Christians, admonished to get excited when all of these things *"come to pass."* We are told to *"look up and lift up your heads; for your redemption draweth nigh,"* Luke 21:28.

My beloved friend, these are the most exciting days in all of history! You and I have been chosen of God, (*Psalm 139*), and it is my belief that we will be alive at the coming of the Lord Jesus Christ. How wonderful the privilege to be placed in the service of God as a weapon in His Hands through prayer, to speak these glorious truths and to experience the beginning of the coming persecution of His saints! In going through these trials, we shall know the profound relationship of His Grace as it consumes us. We shall experience the triumph, the *"joy unspeakable,"* that comes with the transfer of our lives to His, to live within His Faith, and to know the working of the Spirit that has been experienced by few in past history.

Then, as we *"walk through the valley of the shadow of death,"* we will understand dying grace, (*Psalm 23:4,*) as the believers did in Rome. Tied to stakes with wood burning at their feet, the stench of their burning flesh filled the nostrils of the Romans who had assembled to watch the Christians burn and scream in terror. History says their (Romans') ears were never acquainted with the sounds of fear from the mouths of those dying, but heard only the glorious declarations of praise to God, as burning human torches sang their way into the presence of Jesus Christ. The result of joyous breaking will come as you enter the door of death. It is actually the portal to glory. As the songwriter says, "Wonderful Grace of Jesus, greater than all our sins."

In this chapter, we're going to take a Biblical look at breaking as a means to maturity. Someone well said, "When troubles come you are reduced to the level of what you believe." Another statement says, "Blessings are sometimes wrapped in the rags of sorrows." Add these statements to the Scripture which reminds us that God purifies our pursuit by failure, in that He not only allows our defeat, but engineers it to empty us of all self-sufficiency, all self-satisfaction, as He creates evil. Then, in the midst of the conflict, He brings us to brokenness through calamity as we surrender in total abandonment. From that position, we experience results that are then performed only by God's Spirit through us. God says in *Psalm 4:1*, *"Thou hast enlarged me when I was in distress."* Do you remember going through a breaking, and in the end you came out on the other side with a greater relationship to God? Do you recall in the event that your faith was brought into a new and more profound dimension? In fact, in the midst of it you were introduced to the wondrous mysteries of God, (*Colossians 1:26-27*).

God says, in *Psalm 119:71*, *"It is good for me that I have been afflicted that I might learn your statutes."* Through these deep experiences, the Scripture, *"Learn of Me"* becomes a reality. God's "school of learning" is taught through the midst of tears. When God responds, by holy awe you stand saying, "That's God working in and through my life." At the same time, your flesh submits to His parental authority as you yield to God as your Father. You will enjoy His loving relationship and seek constantly His fellowship in application. From there you will learn the truth of *I Thessalonians 5:16*, which says, *"Rejoice evermore."* Also, *Psalm 102:17* says, *"He will regard the prayer of the destitute, and not despise their prayer."*

"O Lord, drench us with humility," was the plea of Oswald Chambers, one of the most poignant and searching writers of the twentieth century. In one of his books, <u>He Shall Glorify Me</u>, he has much to say about this most needed attribute.

> "Our Lord begins where we would never begin, at the point of human destitution. The greatest blessing a man ever gets from God is the realization that if he is going to enter into His Kingdom, it must be through the door of destitution. Naturally, we do not want to begin there, that is why the appeal of Jesus is of no use until we come face to face with realities; then the only one worth listening to is the Lord.
>
> We learn to welcome the patience of Jesus only when we get to the point of human destitution. It is not that God will not do anything for us until we get there, but that He cannot. God can do nothing for me if I am sufficient for myself. When we come to the place of destitution spiritually, we find the Lord waiting, and saying, 'If any man thirst, let him come unto me and drink.'"

Moving on to *I Thessalonians 5:18*, you become foundationally set upon the truth of this verse as it says, *"In everything give thanks: for this is the will of God in Christ Jesus concerning you."* Also, there is a profound verse in *Hebrews 10:32* that says, *"But call to remembrance the former days, in which, after ye were illuminated, ye endured a great fight of afflictions."* In essence, what God is saying to us is that when we are learning a truth, in order to make it a reality within us, God will put us in the midst of conflict, establishing first the presence of that truth. Then, as we seek to apply it to the circumstance, we become alive to its reality and power.

In order for God to marry Truth to my life over these years, it seems that I've had to live out every book I've ever written. I wrote a book some years ago on finance, titled <u>The Scriptural Way To Get Out Of Debt</u>. In the process of researching and writing the book, God placed me into some very trying situations where I had to depend on Him to be the total answer. From that place we learned the truth of tithing. We learned not to make a debt, but to believe God for everything in His Will. From there, He led us into the joys of giving in order to receive. In fact, we were broken into transferring ownership of everything we had back to God. It was hard to go through, but how wonderful the place with Him now.

I later wrote a book regarding critical and negative confession. He then placed us into circumstances where we, though misunderstood, were not allowed to even defend ourselves. Through it we have learned to <u>K.Y.M.S.</u> or <u>KEEP YOUR MOUTH SHUT!</u>

IT COMES WITH THE TERRITORY

Now remember, in *Hebrews 10:32*, God says, *"Call to remembrance former days, in which, after ye were illuminated, ye endured a great fight of affliction;"* I remember in the late 1960's, I began praying that God would do whatever it would take in my life to break me. My ministry seemed to have no lasting effect in the churches. Needless to say, as I sought Him in this, He immediately began the process. The first thing was to place me at the feet of some great men of God who taught the transformed life. In essence, their message was that I must stay filled with the Spirit, that through individuals, God might conduct the Will of God, by the Power of God, that the Glory of God might be in evidence, not only to us, but through us to others. Again, you must understand that all true ministry is God's Spirit to and through our lives.

As I began to listen to and then read the writings of saints whom God had anointed, my heart was desperately burdened to go on. I experienced with Him in Switzerland the filling of the Holy Spirit in 1971. God transformed His Life to mine in a way that I had never known. I wept for days at the joyous presence of Jesus Christ that I had known previously in my mind, but had never felt deep in my heart, (even though I was saved). A hunger to know these deeper things of God came as I read the writings of Andrew Murray, George Mueller, Rees Howell, and A. W. Tozier, as well as others who all had a similar broken life before God.

History says from that profound instant in their person, God's Glory began to manifest through their ministries, and it was sovereignly changed from their ministries into Jesus Christ's. Suddenly things began to happen to me that I did not understand. My ministry began to change. My concern became greater for people. I wept that God would use me. Oh, how I begged Him! Then, as He would move through me, I would ask, "Why, God, am I being misunderstood? Why do these people that so loved me at one time seem to be moving away, having nothing to do with me? What about all of these canceled revivals, Father? How am I going to feed my family? Are you through with me? Am I to go into the business world? What do you want me to do?"

Beloved, in the transition of all the worry about the "how's" and the "why's," plus the pleading for His Presence and Intervention, God was creating through calamity a vacuum in my life that only He could fill. The object was to reduce me from the place of self-engineered ministry and righteousness to the total abandonment of my life to His Glory. It was not until later that God opened for me, in my spirit, *Hebrews 10:32*, while I was trying to express my problems to another, wondering what was going on in my life. He then spoke of the fact that this was an engineered process of God to bring me to discipline and obedience.

As I said earlier, until there is a true diagnosis of an illness, proper treatment cannot be made. Self, or pride, was such a part of my total spiritual environment. As I, however, became more illuminated with truth through correction, Bible study, and prayer, there was an even more profound move of God to bring a greater breaking. This can be understood better by looking at another translation of *Hebrews 10:32*. Here it says:

> *"But be ever mindful of the days gone by in which, after you were first spiritually enlightened, you endured a great and painful struggle." (Amplified)*

And then, the next verse says it all:

> *"Partly, whilst ye were made a gazingstock both by reproaches and afflictions; and partly, whilst you became companions of them that were so used."*

How profoundly true this is! Everything that was happening to me was written by God before the foundations of the world. For you see my beloved friend, when I began to be enlightened by the Truth of the Spirit of God working His Ministry through me, and being filled with and walking in the Holy Spirit, I became a gazing stock. I became, as the Amplified says in that verse:

"Publicly exposed to insults and abuse and distress and sometimes claiming fellowship and making common cause with others who were so treated."

Now, I could write a chapter on just that, for this is what happens to the life of the believer who prays to go on. God moves that person to other individuals who have had the same wilderness experience in their lives. As a side light to this, when I would try to sit down and tell others my problems, they would at first laugh at me. My first thought was, "Is this what the Spirit-filled life is all about, rejection from others who have been down the same path?" And then, I would find that they could "out-do" me in stories of having been denied that came after their revelation. My beloved friends, Satan moves the hardest upon righteousness. He controls religion through pride and confusion, but righteousness is God controlling the individual based on His personal Will. How dangerous to the evil one is that kind of person!

I know that it is strange to many people to deal with the issue of brokenness from a joyous place, but my question to you as a Christian is, "Can the devil touch you without permission of God?" Absolutely not. So, as you move through breaking, seeking Him, you've got to understand that your mind set must be from the point of praise. Praise becomes a sword that attacks the accuser, who wants to bring you to such discouragement in the midst of your conflict that you lose sight of all that is God-engineered for your maturity.

You say, "Well, you just don't know my problems. God can't have anything to do with what I am going through." Well, please remember there are two forms of conflict in the life of a Christian. There is the position of chastisement when sin is involved, bringing you back to a place of obedience into the Will of God. And there is the conditional breaking of the Christian through tribulation to develop maturing, so that in the spiral upward he moves to greater faith. The greater the tribulation that you work through in praise, the greater faith you are building inside. The tests of God are always to bring maturity.

I'm reminded of Abraham and his son Isaac, when Abraham was instructed to go and take the life of Isaac in sacrifice. In obedience he did not hesitate. Now that's trust! Do you know the story? He took the animals, the servants, the fire, the wood, the son, plus the sacrificial knife, and made the three-day journey. Upon arriving at the base of the mountain, he told the servants to remain. Then he and Isaac carried the implements of sacrifice and climbed to the top of the mount. As they arrived, the question was asked by Isaac, *"Where is the sacrifice?"* And Abraham said, *"God will provide Himself a lamb..."* He, in obedience, took his son. After laying the wood upon the altar, he prepared him for sacrifice. Upon raising the knife above his head, God stilled his hand. Then, upon God's instructions, Abraham lifted up his eyes and saw in the thicket a ram hung by his horns. Without hesitancy, the son was removed, his bonds were cut that he might be released, and then the ram was sacrificed in a burnt offering.

You say, "Brother Bonner, was there ever fear in the life of this man that his son would die?" In my opinion, there was not, because he had already received a promise from God that this boy's life would produce many lives. It was a test of obedience in that God said, *"I know that thou fearest God,"* (*Genesis 22:12*). This meant that he was in complete reverence to God. In the light of this, the opposite of fear is faith, and in the midst of his tribulation he obeyed, holding onto the promise of God for his son Isaac.

Incidentally, we have the same promise given to us in *Romans 8:28*, where it says, *"and we know that all things work together for good to them that love God, to them who are the called according to His purpose."* And I might add, in the miracle of Abraham and his son, Isaac, we have an insight as to how God works in a test. As Abraham was going up one side of the mountain in his obedience to sacrifice the boy, the ram was coming up the other. During the whole event, God had already provided a way of escape. Always look for God in everything, for He says, *"All things work together,"* and the joy of it is that God has a plan in every matter. How great our God!

Are you serious about going on with the Lord? Do you want God's Spirit to manifest and minister and work through you? *II Corinthians 6:4-10*, says:

> *"But in all things approving ourselves as the ministers of God, in much patience, in afflictions, in necessities, in distresses;"*

Then, it continues as God says:

> *"In stripes, in imprisonments, in tumults, in labors, in watchings, in fastings; by pureness, by knowledge, by longsuffering, by kindness, by the Holy Ghost, by love unfeigned, by the word of truth, by the power of God, by the armour of*

righteousness on the right hand and on the left, by honor and dishonor, by evil report and good report: as deceivers, and yet true; as unknown, and yet well-known; as dying, and, behold, we live; as chastened, and not killed; as sorrowful, yet always rejoicing; as poor, yet making many rich; as having nothing, and yet possessing all things."

You say, "Brother Bonner, am I to go through that?" The Scripture teaches that in the shaking process, (**Hebrews 12:27**), these are the results of maturing with God. They are, in fact, steps up to His Will. Remember, however, the final phrase: **"And yet possessing all things."** Now, to view things from an earthly posture, the whole concept of life is, "live to get."

Recently, I saw a bumper strip that said, "He who dies with the most toys, wins." My heart was grieved in that this is man's whole design to them that are carnal or lost.

I am reminded of a poem by Mary D. James that expresses this completely:

> *Worldings prize their gems of beauty,*
> *Cling to gilded toys of dust,*
> *Boast of wealth and fame and pleasure,*
> *Only Jesus will I trust.*
> *Since mine eyes were fixed on Jesus,*
> *I've lost sight of all beside,*
> *So enchained my spirit's vision,*
> *Looking at the Crucified.*

"What shall it profit a man if he gains the whole world and loses his own soul?" (**Mark 8:36**) My question is, "Do you believe that Jesus Christ is the Son of God? Do you believe that the Bible is the Word of God? Do you have profound revealed knowledge in your spirit that there is a heaven and a hell and an eternity? Do you know that the laying up of treasures in heaven only begins when you give your life and will totally back to God?" From there commences the experience of heaven's adventure here, as you **"walk by faith and not by sight."** God knows the end times that are so rapidly coming. It has to be understood that the person with true ministry will be the individual who has been enlightened, illuminated, and saturated by the Spirit of God, that he might walk in His Will. However, these words are being used today in "new age" teachings. Be careful of the origin of your power.

Over the years, and after many times of preaching and teaching in the area of the spirit-filled life, it is my desire to go on with God. For in the process of being groomed for His Ministry through me, I have been brought back time and again to three verses in the Book of James. I have alluded to them several times in these chapters, but I want you to see them in the true and complete light. How often have I gone back to review these inspired words? I finally memorized them for myself. They held the key to overcoming the negative issues that were being faced in my life. The problems were so far beyond my abilities that I knew there was nothing that could be done by me, physically, emotionally, or by promotion, to work them out. Time and again I have faced situations that I knew were from God, breaking me for His Purpose and Ministry.

The verses are in *James 1:2-4*. I'm going to use the Amplified version of this, in that as I've carefully searched out the translation of these verses, I feel they bear the best description of what God is saying. They begin:

> *"Consider it wholly joyful, my brethren, whenever you are enveloped in or encounter*

trials of any sort, or fall into various temptations. Be assured and understand that the trial and proving of your faith bring out endurance and steadfastness and patience. But let endurance and steadfastness and patience have full play and do a thorough work, so that you may be [people] perfectly and fully developed (with no defects), lacking in nothing."

God begins with a strange statement regarding problems. He says, *"Consider it wholly joyful."* Now, it's one thing to face the issues of tribulation until you can have peace in the matter, having transferred the problem to God. But it is another thing entirely to really get excited when troubles come, for in essence, that's what He is saying. We are literally to be happy when these events transpire.

You say, "Brother Bonner, that is crazy." Essentially, that is so. Crazy, being defined basically, is the inability to control one's rational behavior, being out of your mind. In this case, out of your mind into His, (*Philippians 2:5*). Now, what is rational to the world? Well, it's to be despondent in the midst of trials, and yet God says to us that we are to **"consider it wholly joyful, my brethren, when we are enveloped in or encounter trials of any sort."** Strange! And yet it is a profound truth based on what we are told in the Scriptures.

He commands us to understand that **"all things work together for good."** So, we are to face every trial in a position of praise if we are maturing in Christ. For these are allowed by God to develop the character of Christ and the sufficiency of His Grace in us. We become, as the Bible states, "enveloped" in these tribulations. Remember, Christ was subject to like passions as we are, yet He did not sin. That simply means that

He came face to face with every trial, and through the power of prayer, the Father interjected His Will through His Son's life. Nothing could consume Him.

From the same position, when tribulations or temptations come at us, we are to face these situations in praise, until suddenly the Peace of God consumes our lives. At that point, God becomes sufficient in the matter through His Grace. That's the reason for temptation. In fact, we find in *I Corinthians 10:13*:

> *"There hath no temptation taken you but such as is common to man: but God is faithful, who will not suffer you to be tempted above that ye are able; but will with the temptation also make a way to escape, that ye may be able to bear it."*

Now, do you understand the "why" of Christ's Ministry here and all that He went through? He gave us an avenue of escape through His Grace and by the Power of His Name. As we grow in Christ, we will face greater trials and greater temptations, so that the sufficiency of His Person will become dynamic in the interlude. In the midst of the trial, we, by His Grace become adequate as we take the aggressive position of authority by the Blood, against the adversary who is accusing and attacking. In this strange statement of being joyful or happy, we are to feel joy whenever we face any negative issue, for our response will show the personal level of our maturity. Instead of saying, "Oh no, I don't want this to happen to me," we say, "Hmm, I wonder what God's up to now." Folks, when we face the conflict from praise, by the Power of Grace through the authority of His Name, we begin to grow in the sufficiency of God's Will for our lives, knowing that it is as heaven has written.

Helena Garratt wrote:

"God did not tell His ancient people to remember only the battles fought and the enemies slain, but His Word was, '*Thou shalt remember all the way which the Lord Thy God led thee. ...To humble thee and to prove thee.*' His humblings are as divine as His upliftings; and it is His Hand upon us, breaking us and emptying us, that makes us fit for His use."

Now, in *verse three of James 1*, we have the springboard to becoming joyful in these encounters. For we are told to *"be assured and understand that the trial and proving of your faith..."* Now, let's think for a moment about the reasons for these situations we face in our lives. The purpose is that we be brought into a trial that it might develop and prove our faith. Then, in the midst of the tribulation, we remember that God in the past always made a way for us to escape, once we finally made our stand in praise by faith believing, that the name of Jesus Christ is sufficient in every matter.

We are brought into a new dimension of belief in God, who moves in by His Power, making a way of escape. In the procedure of having been finally brought to the end of ourselves, committed to God we know that the end result of the experience was authored by Him, and that we had nothing to do with it. It was all profoundly God. We progress to a greater working faith and reality of God, praising and adoring His Name and Glory. The whole experience has built within us a new level of living faith because of our obedience in His instruction.

In teaching our spiritual warfare seminars, our goal is to make people understand that it's at the name of Jesus Christ that every knee shall bow. Faith is what you believe that the Name of Jesus Christ will do, having gone to the Father when you use it. And then you pray and begin to get the promises back into your spirit, knowing God has answered. These will come even before you visually see the results of your praying. Through this, your faith becomes even stronger and continues to build. In fact, the greater the faith, the greater the work of God through the Christian. The greater work of God, the greater the breaking and sufficiency of His Grace. Again, "round and round she goes ..."up or down. You choose the way.

And so God initiates tribulation into our lives so that we will, in the final analysis, learn to yield to Him as our only hope. Then, in the midst of that trial, as God supplies, our faith increases as Christ grows even more powerful and more sufficient in us. Herein is the truth of *Galatians 2:20*, the profound statement that the level of your faith is the level of Christ's control in your life. For it says, *"We are to live by the faith of the Son of God,"* (emphasis mine).

A BLOCK IN MY BODY

In the following verse, there are three things that God develops in your life while in the midst of tribulation. Remember that the purpose of your trial is to prove your faith, that Jesus might become completely sufficient in the matter. *I Peter 1:7-9* says:

> *"That the trial of your faith, being much more precious than of gold that perisheth, though it be tried with fire, might be found unto praise and honour and glory at the appearing of Jesus Christ: whom having not seen, ye love; in whom, though now ye see him not, yet*

*believing, ye rejoice with joy unspeakable and
full of glory: receiving the end of your faith,
even the salvation of your souls."*

Oh, how great the Grace of God! But please remember
that all trials are for the proving of your faith. God says in
James 1:3: *"To bring out endurance and steadfastness and
patience."* To begin with, the word "endurance" is a unique
word that simply means "to be able to run the race, until you
have reached the goal."

I am reminded of a situation that happened to me a
number of years ago. I was in a wonderful church. The pastor
ran six miles a day. Now, this pastor was the "covering" for my
ministry, and he was forever on me about running with him, as
was my Sunday School teacher, a very gracious man of God. I
decided, after a great deal of prompting, that I had best consider
this because it was my pastor speaking to me. Now, one of the
great verses in the Bible that I've always enjoyed (based on
thirty-five years of evangelism and a great deal of dining in the
homes of precious people), is one that says **"bodily exercise
profiteth little."** (*I Timothy 4:8*) I realize that at my age,
there has to be exercise in order to keep everything functional
for health's sake. And I do make an effort to do that, even
though I travel to different areas almost weekly. My pastor was
serious about this, so I decided that I would get serious about
physically bringing myself to run with these men.

To get the process started, I thought I would begin a daily
exercise program. In essence, I desired to run a mile the first
day, two miles the second day, three miles the third day, and so
on until my body was conditioned to at least stay up with them.
I felt that in order to do this, I had to be in fashion and have a
pair of jogging togs. These men were so aptly dressed with their
matching shirt, pants, and Reeboks, that I felt that I must at

least reach the designer state and do the same thing. Much to my amazement I had no concept of the cost of this apparel. As I went to a men's store, I found these uniforms were selling for around $50.00 a set. I had to be out of my mind to pay that much money for something I was embarrassed to be seen in anyway, especially at my size and weight.

So I felt that I was reprieved by the Holy Spirit of this particular endeavor. Now, my wife, whose life brought me into commitment to Christ and salvation, loves to shop at any store that has the word "discount" on the marquee. She found one store whose blazing herald invited us to a promise of great savings. I have always contended, (however it did no good), that we could have saved even more if we hadn't gone in. Nevertheless, we went into one of these so-called "discount" establishments. As I passed the men's section, I noticed that on sale were those ridiculous looking Chinese pajamas, complete with a stripe down the side. Everyone at that time was wearing them, not running in them, just wearing them about. I knew, however, that I was safe. Number one, I could afford none of them, and number two, they did not have any in my size: EXW, extra large whale. But just in case God was behind this, I looked at them anyway. Much to my amazement, as well as my chagrin, the first set I looked at was not only on sale at a very reasonable price, but they were extra large/tall, exactly what I needed. In my spirit I said, "O.K., Lord," and bought these, tax included, for less than $12.00. I thought, "This must be God."

Then, with this mandate, I got up early the next morning. Now, when I say early, I'm talking about 4:00 a.m., because of what I looked like dressed in that outfit, strings and all. Needless to say, I was embarrassed. I needed, however, to get that first mile under my belt. Another reason I got up at that time, was to avoid embarrassment from the man across the street, by the name of Russ Culbertson. Russ and Betty had come to a Bible study in my home several months before, and he had been born again. They were dear and precious friends, and still are. The problem was that Russ, two months prior to this, had gone through a by-pass surgery on his heart and was already running over two miles a day. He had several times asked me to run with him. Having seen my size and knowing my eating and traveling habits, there was concern that what happened to his heart would happen to mine. Now, the morning paper was thrown at about 5:00 a.m. in our neighborhood. I knew Russ, an early riser, would be out to get his paper at that time. So I decided, as I said, to start this first day in the dark.

To express to you how little I knew, I put on my running shoes first, and then tried to put on these jogging togs. They would not go on without pulling the shoes off. All of this took five additional minutes. "Time's a wastin," (Al Capp's spelling) as Little Abner used to say. From my house to the first major street and back was exactly one mile. With that thought in mind, I didn't even lock my front door. I knew that I would be back in just a few minutes. As I pulled it shut, I set my face as a flint toward my goal. I took a deep breath and began to run and run. I was soon to discover that I had a mile on my mind, but I had one block in my body. One. At the end of that first block, I stumbled over to the side of the street and grabbed hold of a stop sign. There I was, holding onto that sign with my legs trembling, when suddenly a still small voice began screaming in my head, "You idiot, what are you trying to do, kill us?"

About that time, two or three cars went by containing several of my neighbors. There I stood, with my arms tightly around that stop sign, in those silly blue, (complete with a white stripe,) jogging togs, with those who lived about me looking as they drove to work. Mind you, there is never anyone up that early here and they all left early that one morning. I could hear them in my mind as they went by. "That's the preacher. I wonder what's wrong with him?" I had lived in the neighborhood twelve years at that time. I had tried to show an exemplary life as a witness for Christ. How they stared as they stopped and started off again very slowly! I will never forget it. I tried to smile at them to give them assurance that I was sober, but perhaps a little out of my mind! I sought their sympathy and not their judgment. Oh, well. Praise the Lord! When you are in the ministry and have gone through breaking financially, and you're trusting God for daily provision, and then you remember you've paid almost $12.00 for those togs, you decide you're going to get your money's worth. With my legs trembling, I again reset my flabby face like a flint toward that big street. With my face then in place and trying to convince my body, I began again, this time walking toward my destination. Finally, upon arrival, I turned around and came back, walking as rapidly as I could, until I finally became parallel to that memorable stop sign. (I will always believe God placed it there for my sake.)

Then the tragedy of all tragedies happened. Under the street lamp, at the corner of his yard, stood Russ Culbertson in his bathrobe reaching down to pick up his morning paper. It was one block away. I knew I could not hide behind the small thin pole of that stop sign, so I girded up my loins and anything else I could gird up. I then took a deep breath and began to run. Now, "I picked them up and put them down," all the time holding my breath. I went by him, slosh, slosh, slosh. He said something to me as I jogged by, as he wanted to visit. In response, however, I waved and continued on. I couldn't stop just then, for I had yet to breathe.

Then I ran across that street, down my pebble stone sidewalk, burst in those double doors, ran directly into my den, fell on an orange rug and thought I had died. Seriously, I gasped for breath. Finally, in due season I was able to sit up. I realized it had taken over an hour to go that mile. In fact, it took me three weeks to work up a mile. And then, in my pride, I would start off running from my home and when I got around the corner and out of the visual sight of my wife, I cheated and walked. Oh, the macho image we must keep!

I finally hung those things up. I'd thought many times about framing them as a reminder of those trying times. I do exercise now. I walk, but my running days are over except for a few blocks at a time. The root of my problem then was that I lacked endurance. And it took a while to build that up. I never made it running six miles, or six blocks for that matter.

How many of us as Christians, in the center of tribulation, crumble at the first sight of any kind of conflict? Do you realize this is what God is referring to in *James 1:3*? He is saying to us, Biblically, that we must, in the midst of our conflict, so walk with the Spirit of God that in the process of it, these tribulations build strength into our spiritual bodies, bringing out endurance. It means that we must stay in the race or battle until it is won, and then go with God in these matters of conflict until His Grace is sufficient and His Power becomes the majesty of our authority in every situation.

Now, the second step to spiritual maturity is also found in that verse. It is the place of "steadfastness." God states, in His Word, that we are to: *"Be ye steadfast, immovable, always abounding in the work of the Lord,"* (*I Corinthians 15:58*). He also says, *"Stand fast therefore in the liberty wherewith Christ hath made us free, and be not entangled again with the yoke of bondage,"* (*Galatians 5:1*).

God, through tribulation, directs us through the growth process so that no matter what the conflict is, the sufficiency of God's Grace is within us and that we can, if we will, stand in the midst of any problem in praise, knowing that the Will of God is being performed through our lives, (*Romans 8:28*). And finally, in *James 1:3*, there is a word that brings out all kinds of emotions in the lives of people, and that is "patience". How many of us are patient about everything except waiting?

The story of my life is impatience! I knew that great victory had found its beginning place in my being, and had made an inroad, when I could sit in the car more than three minutes without honking the horn for my wife to come. I've never figured out how she and I can start for the door at the same time, everything ready to go, and somehow lose her between the door and the car. It is beyond me. Yet, beloved, I am learning patience. It has not been an easy virtue to learn. It has not been something that has come simply, but only by Grace. To get where I am momentarily has taken a battle through praise. I cannot stand to be late. I must be early. Even in meetings, I am usually walking through the building in prayer before anyone else comes. Waiting, to me, is not a quality, but a test of my praise quotient. So, needless to say, the battle for this emotion has been earnestly fought for, and not bravely won, for the battle still rages within. I can safely say, however, that I am not where I need to be, but I'm better than I was. Ah, patience. With it is feigned peace on the outside and "bah-humbug" on the inside! God is breaking me. I am progressing forward with creeping violence, such as cold honey pouring from a jar, or as one in the sea of self, trying to run in water up to his neck. "O wretched man ..."

There is a wonderful verse that explains God's Heart in the "why" of conflict. It is found in *Romans 5:3-5*:

> *"And not only so, but we glory in tribulations also: knowing that tribulation worketh of patience; And patience, experience; and experience, hope: And hope maketh not*

ashamed, because the love of God is shed abroad in our hearts by the Holy Ghost which is given unto us."

In reality, God is saying that the activity of tribulation has been the exercise of God's Will in order to bring us into servitude. This trip in my life is not easy and may I say not over. I still have much to learn, but how great our God! In fact, I am in the beginning stages of His planned change for my life bringing me into the image of Christ. But for it to happen, I must continue to pray to be broken.

LET TROUBLES COME

Let's look again at *James 1:4*. Here is an action on our part to be able to go on with God. If I ask you the question, "Do you want to belong to God and go on with Him?" You would, very likely, say, "Oh, yes, Brother Bonner, more than anything else in this world." Well, herein is the position of this verse:

"But let endurance and steadfastness and patience have full play and do a thorough work, so that you may be [people] perfectly and fully developed (with no defects) lacking in nothing."

Now, let's take a hard look at this. God says to us that we are to run the race. We are to do the mile, and then two miles, and then three miles as we develop endurance through the experience of tribulation and breaking. Then, when troubles come, we will not find ourselves in depression, discouragement, dejection, or devastation of character and faith. In fact, in the midst of it all, we will be able to excitedly face every issue in praise. Then we will know that God is all powerful, operating in our decision of faith as he develops within us the birthmark and ministry of the Lord Jesus.

Let troubles come, and in the process, you will become praise-full in the midst of them. You will be developed to a stronger place, able then to run the complete race. Then, as God becomes sufficient in one situation after the other in your life, you are capable of taking in more tribulation, thereby becoming steadfast upon the rock of faith, and, finally, patient in waiting on God. You will be as a stone being battered by the highest of all waves, brought on by the hammering of the strongest wind. But you'll remain immovable and without dent when you face your issues in praise. Again, be "**steadfast, immovable,**" which incidentally has its foundation or cornerstone laid in total peace. Let God continue the work in your life. Let Him finish His business in you as you praise Him, no matter what is happening, for His Grace is sufficient.

From that place, you will operate in the Glory of His Being. Again, get excited when troubles come, remembering that when you find your Christian walk being melted by the heat of anger, frustration, and tribulation, be patient for all things to work together for good. Praise until the end, and you will see the hand of God. Understand that man can't do anything but kill you, but they can't kill you except when God gets ready. Never forget that He is still in control. This is the "stuff" from which intercessors are made. It is "wonderful, the Grace of Jesus."

Now, in essence, all of these verses in James come together in this last line:

"But let endurance and steadfastness and patience have full play. That we may be a people perfectly and fully developed, with no defects, lacking nothing." (Amplified)

God is saying, through this writer, to let Him finish His Work. Pray that He will break you. Let Him do what needs to be done.

At this point, consider the illustration of a "shakedown cruise" for any Navy ship coming out of manufacturing. The ship completed and placed in the hands of a very special crew of officers and men. They are trained to do all they can to cause the ship to break down. They take it to deep water before it ever becomes a ship of the line. They will then proceed at top speed forward and throw it into reverse. Those in the engine room answer the helm. This throws it abruptly in reverse as the drive shafts find themselves being pulled under great stress and rotated in a different way. You say, "Brother Bonner, what is the object of this?" It is to make sure that, in the midst of battle, that ship can stop and reverse its screws without breaking its shaft.

Then they will take it top speed and maneuver it to the left. When the steel plates on the sides become strained from the water pressure underneath, they will then turn it to the right. They will continue to do this over and over to see if they can pop a plate or spring a leak, that it might be repaired, strengthened, and be made conditionally ready, so that in the midst of battle, that ship will be able to give full and complete service to those using it, without breaking down. It is a must before any conflict.

Again, this is called a "shakedown cruise." In like manner does God place us into tribulations and trials, so that we, in the midst of battle, finally submit to the Power of the Holy Spirit, and are able to win. It is a joyful place to join God in battle through prayer and patience, and to be able in the long run to hold together by God's Grace and Power. That's what it means to be "one with Christ" in our lives. For we are to allow brokenness to have full play, that through the breakings, a thorough work might be accomplished, as these men who control the ship out at sea. They are trying, through tribulation, to do everything they can to break it down, finding the weakness in the structure that it might be repaired. In the future, based on the damage-control and repair, it would be a powerful entity to maintain the sovereignty of the land, (*Hebrews 12:27*).

So it is with us in the midst of tribulation. We are brought to a place of being as it says in *James 1:4*, *"people perfectly and fully developed,"* or in other words " a conquering of our problems by praise." We are brought from that place to a greater building of faith. Then we will have *"no defects, lacking in nothing."* Thank God for this last line because it must be understood, beloved, that when you are in God's Grace and Power, regardless of your circumstance, the sufficiency of His Being is so formidable that where you are is where He is in you, based on your joy in the matter. And furthermore, He is supplying everything to meet that need. How great our God! We are lacking in nothing. <u>Nothing</u>. Please understand that this is a learned place in the life of the Christian, who, by experience, has come to the position of the sufficiency of God's Grace in his life.

Memorize and store in your spirit *Psalm 4:1*: *"Thou hast enlarged me when I was in distress."* Then, *Psalm 119:71*: *"It is good for me that I have been afflicted; that I might learn thy statutes,"* and *Hebrews 5:8*: We learn as Jesus did, *"though he were a Son, yet learned he obedience by the things which he suffered;"* It is wonderful that when we go through the adventure of adversity, we come out ultimately in God's Will and Service.

Helena Garratt, with her two sisters, left a comfortable home in beautiful surroundings to go out to Africa where the African Evangelistic Band was formed. She writes:

"As we draw nearer to God, and better understand His ways, we learn to make records according to His Mind. We begin to count His humiliations, His testings, His chastenings, as our most cherished spiritual experiences. The saint who has had the best year in God's sight is not the one who has had an easy path, or has achieved the highest success; not the one whose praises filled the lips of men, but the one who has known the deepest humblings in the Presence of the Highest One, and who has bowed lowest at His Feet. The Lord Jesus said, *'Whosoever shall humble himself ... the same is greatest in the Kingdom of Heaven.'*" (*Matthew 18:4*)

"His over-throw heaped happiness upon him; for then, and not till then, he felt himself and found the blessedness of being little," (Shakespeare). Pray to be broken. It is truly the abundant life.

CHAPTER EIGHT

BROKENNESS -- A GIFT FROM GOD

"When I am weak, then am I strong," (*II Corinthians 12:10*). The older I get, the less I know. I used to know it all. If I didn't know it, I had a library that would give me trusted information from authors who were highly regarded in the denomination of which I was part. These authors were the "last word" on every truth. I constantly sought light as I studied the commentaries and writings of other men's scriptural revelations. I was "ever searching." I have since discovered, however, as years of my Christian life have rolled by, a startling realization, and that is, everything is Jesus Christ.

Several years ago I was asked to speak at a conference in Fort Worth, Texas. Hundreds of pastors would attend that meeting. I wanted therefore, to be as Biblically articulate as I could. At the same time, I wanted to give them quality information filled with depth, meaning, and life, something life-changing before they went back to their churches. I was also very desirous to show my preaching ability, my academics, and the wisdom I had gained over the years. Also in the back of my mind was the thought that some of these pastors might want to invite me to preach a meeting in their churches in the future. God, however, wasn't having anything to do with what I wanted. My problem was that instead of putting together a message packed with one-liners and jokes, I was continually seeking God as to what to say. Over the many weeks, I prayed and sought the face of the Lord for a message, and all I could receive in my spirit was the word "Jesus."

I assured my Father that I was going to preach Jesus, and

that He would be the accentuation of all information that I would give. But I still felt that these men needed the blessing of experiencing my learned ability. What an opportunity! From the very beginning of preparation, the heavens were brass. No word. No presence of God. As the day was getting closer, I was getting more and more frantic. I could put a message together and could sprinkle it with prose, poetry, and humor, but after these numbers of years, I had decidedly become fanatic. I continued to beg the Lord for a word. Again, in my spirit, all I could hear as I prayed was the precious name of "Jesus." "Preach Jesus."

So, as time was depleting, my heart was desolate. I began to finally face the deadline by seeking God desperately for a message. I sat down with the Bible and opened to passages about Jesus. Once God, through discipline, had brought my discouraged mind to complete hopelessness in my own ability, and helplessness in trying to discern His Will without prayer, He began to lay before me what He wanted to say.

Martin Luther wrote, "Never are men more unfit than when they think themselves most fit, and best prepared for their duty; never more fit, than when most humbled and shamed under a sense of their unfitness."

As I prayed, I was led to start in **Galatians 2:20**, about the Faith of Christ. As I began to meditate on this, I was overwhelmed that faith was not an experience, it was a Person. His name is Jesus Christ. It electrified my heart! Suddenly, a focus came of what this verse meant, and I studied faith from a different view. No longer did I hear from the outside-in, but from the inside-out. He is our faith, for we are to *"live by the faith of the Son of God."*

Then I was led to the word "love," and discovered again

that love was not an experience. It is the Person of Christ coming alive in us, for when He is Lord by a desperate desire, (He is Lord of all regardless), then hearts are yielded to Him through breaking. When we labor to enter into rest, the unlovely become lovely. We are overwhelmed by compassion to the point that our hearts are changed. Love is not an experience, but a Person.

From the revelation of **Galatians 2:20**, I became engulfed with the study of the word "peace." We are given the Biblical description that He is Peace, not only the Prince of Peace, but the activity of Peace, for the Scripture says, **"Peace I leave with you, my Peace."** It exploded in my heart that peace was not an experience to be sought. It was the Person, Jesus Christ, alive in me!

It abruptly became apparent to me that all that we try to apply to our lives by principle is not principal at all; it is a Person. It is Jesus, "Christ in You.". From that moment on eschatology seemed to be secondary. I agree that end-time things are important, but the total message is Jesus Christ. The only hope to all, and in all, is Him. Many times, as we preach the soon-coming of Christ, we become infatuated by more and more information about the miracle of the return. Soon our eyes become focused on the present, rather than on the Person of Christ. For Him to be central, we must seek Him constantly. The same applies to miracles. As we chase the manifestation of God rather than the Man, we're led to events where great crowds come looking for the power, rather than the Person. They become enamored by the arena. This was displayed in the time of Christ as the multitudes followed Him everywhere to see the healing and deliverance. And yet, because the Holy Spirit was not residing within, they abandoned Him at His death. In the light of this, as the world sinks into the sunset of history, the church continues to dissipate and disintegrate because the message is not the Man, but a plan. In the process of building religious bodies, as well as "user-friendly churches," we have lost contact with the reality of the Person of Christ within. So the effort is to get people involved in activities rather than in a relationship with the Holy Spirit who was given to conform us to the Image of Christ. Consequently, there are no tears of brokenness, and where there is no brokenness, there is no true ministry.

GOING, GOING, GONE

Future historians, if there be any, will look at what once was a Christian nation that died because the Church lost its place by becoming involved with the business of doing things like the world. They became caught up in the busy-ness of propagation that brought to a dying planet a watered down, compromising Gospel that leavened its truths with error. It has become the sand of which most religious foundations are now placed upon. Needless to say, as time has shown, some are sinking and some are already gone. These churches have traded activity for prayer, and compromise for conviction. They are now meeting the people where they are, rather than where Christ is. Consequently, one complete generation of young people has been lost to value systems that have been coordinated by the demonic, calling evil good and good evil, and having no use for God and His Christ.

We now face the acceleration of the demise and disintegration of the world's first truly foundationally Christian nation, whose very beginning was a harvest of laws and rights of the persons who sought God in deep brokenness in prayer. America was birthed by prayer and will die by religion, as have most nations in history. America's transitions began with Holy God and ended with "mother earth," or better said, "new age wicca," or witchcraft.

As the auctioneer declares at the end of a sale, "Going, Going, Gone," so are the traditional values. They are not just going, but are already gone. Not going, but gone are the principles of righteousness. Not going, but gone is the *"hope of glory."* You say, "Brother Bonner, what can I do? Is there no hope?" No, beloved, there is no hope in what man can do. We are now to the place in history where something profound has to happen that it will stop the world in its tracks. It will take something so explosive that as lightning destroys the darkest night, so must the brightness of Truth come to the hearts of those who are dead in trespasses and sins. There has to be an eruption of God's Glory into the reality of where we are and the Holy Spirit's revelation of what is really going on in the spiritual world. It, however, cannot come in what we are doing today. Very few are interceding with God's burden upon them, and it will take His burden for His Glory to fall. We must see what God sees in order to intercede, bringing His power into the world.

Brokenness is a way of life. Through it God raises up His people for His Purpose and Ministry. In the Old Testament, you will find a constant presence of God with His people as He directed His Purpose for them. When they turned their backs on His will, He would bring them into bondage and captivity, that through this purging of fire might come a purification of their value systems. They eventually cried out to God with a broken and contrite spirit, fully abandoning themselves to His Will. The Prodigal returns ... again and again.

While in bondage or captivity, their sacrifices were to no avail. Their prayers, though with much pleading, had no effect on the hearing of God, (*Joel 2:12-13*). However, they became so desolate of heart that through the door of discouragement and into the place of despair, and through true tears of remorse of their sins, they finally humbled themselves before God. He then ceased their wandering, reaffirmed His relationship, and restored them as a nation. He also re-established their righteousness and brought focus back upon who they were. They belonged to God. As Christians, when broken, we become what we really are through His Life in us and through us. It's life's greatest experience.

Again, without brokenness, there is no true ministry of God's Holy Spirit. For He shines only through the cracks. We find a tremendous example of this in David's life and the difference of his praying based on the events that transpired. Before David fell through his intimacy with Bathsheba, his cry was:

"The Lord is near unto those who are of a broken heart, and saved such as be of a contrite spirit," (*Psalm 34:18*).

Now, listen to this same man who then reaped the rewards of his unrighteousness, having the sword over his head as he cried after his fall:

"The sacrifices of God are a broken spirit. A broken and a contrite heart, oh God, you will not despise," (*Psalm 51:17*).

Now, the word "brokenness" literally means (in the Hebrew language) to "splinter into pieces". It becomes a reality in our lives when we are broken and contrite in our spirit, and come into His presence in true prayer, thereby having our innermost being detonated with the Glory of His Life. In that glorious experience, we are overwhelmed with contrition because of the perverseness of what and who we really are. This is the "contrite" that God speaks of in His Word. When man stands in the righteous presence of God, he is devastated over his own sin.

As we stated in earlier chapters, I have made a study of many of God's heroes whose lives, over the centuries, have literally mirrored the Ministry of Christ. In reading, one evident factor surfaced in every biography. Sometime in each believer's life, there was a cataclysmic situation in which God was the only hope. Each one completely threw himself on Him, to the point that God's Grace became totally sufficient in the tragic matter. From that place, they all rose from the ashes and were formed by the Power of God into willing, obedient servants, pursuing after righteousness. As a result, their ministries were birthed. Only true brokenness in life will bring true ministry. Thomas Kelly stated it well when he wrote:

> "But the humility of the God-blinded soul endures only so long as we look steadily at the sun. Growth in humility is a measure of our growth in the habit of the God ward-directed mind. And he only is near to God who is exceedingly humble. The last depths of holy and voluntary poverty are not in financial poverty, important as that is; they are in poverty of spirit, in meekness and lowli-ness of soul."

In my own life, there are three verses that I have prayed over the years, begging God for the events in my life to be structured upon the foundation of these truths. I urge you who are serious with God, who desire the joyous walk and the victory of that relationship of righteousness, you who are willing seek with all hope the transformed life, (*Romans 12:1-2*), to begin to pray *Isaiah 57:15, 66:2*, and *Philippians 3:10*. What you are doing is praying Scripture back to God, asking for this to be applied to your life. It is the beginning of a glorious walk. It will be His through you, for here we find testimony of God that He will dwell in the high and holy place with him who has a contrite and humble spirit.

The word "contrite" has a little different meaning from brokenness. It means "to be crushed." You say, "Brother Bonner, I don't know if I want to be crushed." As one minister said to me recently, "I don't want to make that trip. I am afraid of what God might do to me or my family." This is an accusation of Satan. My questions to you are, "Did you have an earthly father that you loved and trusted, and have wonderful memories of? Did you submit your youthful life to him? Did he not care for you? Did he not love you? Did he not have a desire for your future well being?" If you could trust your earthly father, how much more could you trust our precious *"Father which art in heaven!"* Can you imagine the quality of love that He had in that He so loved us that He gave His Son that we could have everlasting life? As your father prepared for you a home with the working of His hands, has not God done the same for eternity with the price of His Son? The Scripture says, **"God is love,"** and in the giving of His Son He proved His true personification. He loves you and will take care of you. I know firsthand this wondrous truth.

Now, if you want to walk in the place of victory or joy where Jesus is everything, then you must come to where God is. As I have stated, religion is an effort to operate in co-motion, based on pro-motion, to bring emotion, with great hope that God will join into the man-planned event. But, True Christianity is the thrusting of ourselves into the Will of God, begging to be broken while praying for His Will to be done, that His Kingdom might come in our lives. Christ, in his earthly ministry, was the most humble of all servants. His total life was in the living and dying for others. Therefore, Christ today becomes alive and continues His Ministry in us through our desired breaking and in the presenting of our bodies, a living sacrifice.

In **Philippians 2**, we find that *"Christ humbled Himself."* Gerhard Tersteegen, a contemporary of Wesley and

Whitefield, writes:

> "We cannot humble ourselves, but must let ourselves be humbled. Christ humbles us by His guidance of us and by His Spirit; and thus makes us acceptable to God in and through him."

Then the process of contriteness, (being ground to powder), begins. The process begins with God adding the water of the Holy Spirit to our dust, shaping us on the potter's wheel through the events of His Will. We, then, begin to take the form of His pre-plan for our lives, (*Ephesians 2:10*). Next, we are fired in the kiln of tribulation. Praise, faith, and ministry are brought out of the situation. The results will reflect our maturing, tempered, and resolute desire to righteousness as He pours within our expanded vessel the "water of The Holy Spirit" to overflowing. It must also be understood that if you are tried by fire here, your works will not burn there, (*I Corinthians 3:12-15*). Oh, how great our God! Is there anyone who would be willing to say, "Father, in the name of Jesus, whatever it takes in my life?" The Scripture says in *James 4:6*, *"God resisteth the proud, but giveth grace to the humble."*

Harvey says:

> "Richard Baxter, the Puritan preacher and writer, labored under a burden of ill health all of his life. He attributed much of his usefulness to the fact that he ministered as a dying man to dying men, with a constant sense of eternity before him. He wrote: 'Communion with God will keep men low, and that lowliness will promote their communion. When a man is used to being much with God and taken up with the study of His glorious attributes, he abhors himself in dust and ashes. And that self-

abhorrence is his best preparative to obtain admittance to God again.

Therefore, after a soul-humbling day or in times of trouble, when the soul is lowest, it useth to free access to God and savor most of life above. The delight of God is in him that is poor and of a contrite spirit, and trembleth at (His) Word; and the delight of such a soul is in God. Where there is mutual delight, there will be freest admittance, heartiest welcome, and frequent converse ...

O Christian, if thou wouldst live continually in the Presence of the Lord, lie in the dust, and He will then take you up. Learn of Him to be meek and lowly, and thou shalt find rest unto your soul. Otherwise, thou shalt be like the troubled sea, when it cannot rest, whose waters cast up mire and dirt. Instead of these sweet delights in God, thy pride will fill thee with perpetual disquiet.

As he that humbleth himself as a little child shall be greatest in the Kingdom of Heaven, so shall he now be greatest in the foretaste of that kingdom.'"

The rest of *Isaiah 57:15* then tells us that God will revive the spirit of the humble or broken and revive the heart of the contrite ones. Not only will they come to life as they have never experienced, but will also come alive to the Person of Christ in peace and to the Power of His name and to the Glory of His Life. Then will the true ministry of Christ's Life and journey be through them to others. It is the Christ in you.

Robert Murray McCheyne was a godly young minister who had organized over 30 prayer meetings in his large parish in Perth, Northern Scotland. He wrote: "I charge you, be clothed with humility. Let Christ increase; let man decrease. This is my constant prayer for myself and you."

When laid aside by sickness, McCheyne was sorely tested and wrote:

> "Paul asked, what wilt thou have me do? And it was answered, 'I will show him what great things he must suffer for my name's sake.' Thus, it may be with me. I have been too anxious to do great things. The lust of praise has ever been my besetting sin, and what more befitting school could be found for me than that of suffering alone, away from the eye and ear of man."

He was being prepared for what was to follow, when, because of ill health, he was sent by the Synod of the Church of Scotland with a party of other ministers to search out the condition of the Jews abroad. "I sometimes think," he said, "that a great blessing may come to my people in my absence. Often God does not bless us when we are in the midst of our labors, lest we shall say, 'my hand and my eloquence have done it.' He removes us into silence and then pours down a blessing so that there is no room to receive it; so that all that see it cry out, 'It is the Lord.'" (Harvey)

Again, one person can bring revival. Historically, every great move of God began in the heart of one broken person in prayer.

In *Isaiah 66:2*, we again are told that our fear, (Reverential Awe), should be in the Lord. He will look for and use the individual that is poor and of a contrite spirit. The word "poor" can be matched in the beatitudes. In *Matthew 5:3*, the Scripture says, *"Blessed are the poor in spirit, for theirs is the kingdom of heaven."* Here the word "poor" is translated as an individual who becomes "humble, rating himself insignificant. That person is "happy", spiritually prosperous, filled with life, joy, and satisfaction in God's favor and salvation." (Amplified) The key to all life, therefore, is found in God's way by giving ourselves first to Him and then unto others by His Will, or better said, Him through us.

An evident sign of not being contrite before the Lord is to desire recognition in the doing of good works. This recognition could manifest in accolades or finances. It has been said, "You either possess your possessions or they possess you." Real victory, however, comes when your eyes are not upon the world's system of receiving, but on the Kingdom of God that says "give." The true, broken individual will be a person who readily and with excitement, lives for others, rather than for himself. When Christ is truly living His Life through a person, his joy will be in giving. I might suggest a prayer to pray to God in the name of Jesus Christ: "Lord, reveal me to me as You see me." And if this prayer comes from a broken, contrite spirit with desire to mature, you will truly, at that point in life, enter into the greatest experience that is ever known to man: to see yourself as God sees you, which brings true repentance, clearing your life of demonic strongholds. It will take that for Christ to live His Life through you.

There is a poem by George MacDonald that would apply here:

"The man who was Lord of fate,
Born in an ox's stall,
Was great because He was much too great
To care about greatness at all.
You long to be great; you try,
You feel yourself smaller still,
In the Name of God let ambition die,
Let Him make you what He will."

Finally, *Isaiah 66:2* says, *"And trembleth at my word."* Oh, what a delight to open the Word of God and read it, and suddenly have it speak to your spirit a truth as written in the Scripture. It is like a well that springs up inside, bringing the reality of all that He is. These are moments of true grace as God's Holy Spirit reveals to our spirit that the Scripture is really Jesus Christ. What moments of joy unspeakable!

Have you experienced them? If so, I ask you to reflect back to those moments and recall if there was not some circumstance that drove you to God in need, whether it was in tribulation or in Bible study as you desired deeply to feast on His Word. I believe you will find that always before joyous revelation, there is desolation that brings desperation, which finally leads you through the door of restoration. The other verse that I pray is *Philippians 3:10*. I have mentioned it a number of times to this point. Oh, to have within us the true, working Image of Christ. What joy to finally come home, as the prodigal in the breaking of his rebellion, and find the father waiting. Our Father is waiting. Come home, believer, that He can accomplish His work in your life to His Glory. He's waiting and wanting to use you. When He does, oh, the "joy unspeakable!"

John Fletcher, the Vicar of Madeley, would lie prostrate on the floor whole nights, pleading with God to subdue the strong man and keep him meek and lowly. In a letter to Charles Wesley, he bewails his lack:

> "A few days ago, the Lord gave me two or three lessons on the subject of poverty of spirit, but alas, how have I forgotten them! I saw, I felt, that I was entirely void of wisdom and virtue. I was ashamed of myself and I could say with a degree of feeling, which I cannot describe, 'I do nothing, have

nothing, am nothing; I crawl in the dust.' I could then say what Gregory Lopez was enabled to say at all times: 'There is no man of whom I have not a better opinion than of myself.' I could have placed myself under the feet of the most atrocious sinner, and have acknowledged him for a saint in comparison of myself.

If ever I am humble and patient, if ever I enjoy solid peace of mind, it must be in this very spirit. Ah! Why do I not actually find these virtues; because I am filled with self-sufficiency, and am possessed by self-esteem, which blinds me and hinders me from doing justice to my own demerits. Oh! Pray that the Spirit of Jesus may remove these scales from my eyes forever, and compel me to retire into my own nothingness."

He wrote:

> "Lord, Thou doest Thy Grace impart,
> Poor in spirit, meek in heart.
> I shall, as my Master, be,
> Rooted in humility.
> Now, dear Lord, that Thee I know,
> Nothing will I seek below.
> Aim at nothing great or high,
> Lowly both in heart and eye."

John Fletcher knew the Man.

CHAPTER NINE

THE CONSENT OF TRIBULATION

In giving God total union with our spirit, we desire, at all costs, to grow and mature in Him. By humility we are led of the Holy Spirit, which conforms us to the Image of Christ from the inside. Then the Ministry of Christ begins through us, reflected externally. Ministry begins by brokenness in prayer; it is God's Power through man. As I shared earlier, we are earthen vessels to be broken, that Christ's Light may shine through us. Any ministry without Christ's Will is perpetrated through the flesh based on the individual's desire for success. Remember, this is the activity of religion. When we are broken, however, the Spirit of God that dwells within us as a light, begins to shine through the cracks. For we, as body, soul, and spirit, then have the Holy Spirit in our spirits, bringing through our lives the Ministry of God's Power.

Now, this will occur only when you fight spiritually to walk with God. You must make a daily application of the cross to your life, as Paul, who stated, *"I am crucified with Christ,"* (*Galatians 2:20*). The verse continues by stating, *"... nevertheless I live, yet not I, but Christ that liveth in me."* It is only from the place of crucifixion or resurrected life that we extend His Will. As I have stated several times, (and it must be indelibly placed in your heart), that when you stand before God, you're not going to be rewarded for what you have done in the name of Jesus Christ, but for what Christ has done through you in His Name. I would to God that you ask Him for the truth of that statement. God breaks through to develop your life by your choosing to be broken, desperately desiring the ministry that He has designed for you. He continues then to mature your character through tribulation, and your spiritual growth barometer is how you react to it, (*Ephesians 5:20*).

If you are out of God's Will, He brings to your life chastisement in order to get your attention. Scourging is applied if you will not adhere to chastisement. On the other hand, the believer walking with God will experience discipline while looking for the purpose of that transition as he is taken to a new level of ministry. The question of the maturing in this process of change will be, "God, what are you saying to me? What are you trying to perform through my life?"

And so, as one stands in praise in the midst of his problems, persecutions, and pressures, he becomes designed by God for the working of His Will. He becomes the instrument of God's Glory. Tribulation is not designed to hurt you, for, "*All things work together for good, for those that love God and are called according to His purpose,*" (*Romans 8:28*). So, you must get excited when troubles come. As I stated earlier, this is God ringing your doorbell. He wants to come in.

Again, I have never met anyone profoundly used of God in ministry that has not gone through great tribulation in order that the Spirit of God would become the interworking of his life due to his self-abandonment and obedience to Christ. The same is true for those of whom I have read. As I have gone through the journals written by many who have studied the manifestations of God through the lives of men who ministered in a powerful way, all who wrote of them said that these were broken before God in their spirit man. The Bible established this in *II Corinthians 4:6-12*. Here He tells us that we are literally to be submitted to the Spirit of God and that He, through us, will bring the "*knowledge of the Glory of God in the face of Jesus Christ.*" For in a broken state, that light that dwells within us will "*shine out of darkness.*" It has literally shined in our hearts. This treasure is in earthen vessels, that the excellency of the power may be of God and not of us. All ministry that is pure ministry is the extension of the Holy Spirit through us, and it comes from that Light that shines within our very beings.

As we move toward the end period of history, **II Corinthians 4:8-10** perhaps we will have the greatest explanation of what we're going to be facing in future days. For it says:

> *"We are troubled on every side, yet not distressed; we are perplexed, but not in despair. Persecuted, but not forsaken. Cast down, but not destroyed. Always bearing about in the body the dying of the Lord Jesus, that the life also of Jesus might be made manifest in our body."*

How profound the statement that we bear in our body the dying of the Lord Jesus! His Power within us becomes His Ministry through us as we reckon ourselves crucified in a daily application of His Spirit in our lives. And when that happens, Christ becomes manifest or present and controls our mortal flesh. *"So then death worketh in us, but life in you,"* *verse 12* continues.

My beloved friend, the greatest single experience, apart from salvation in your life, is when you come to the place that Christ has consumed you and has moved through your body according to His Purpose. But it will never come until, by personal design and desire, you beg to go on with God.

Travailing literally brings the birth of the Will of God in your life. *Galatians 4:19* says, *"My little children of whom I travail in birth again until Christ be formed in you.*" Here Paul gives to us the true insight to intercessory prayer and its place within his life. "Travail" is defined as "strenuous activity that involves difficulty and effort" -- in other words, warfare. He literally fought for them through prayer. He was a true example of a broken man, and it came to his life through a daily yielding of his being to God.

If you want to walk with God, you must get serious. You must pray to be broken before the Lord. It has to be the desire of your heart. Then, in the process of your transformation by pruning, you need to begin to pray for others to be broken. Answered prayer is the only true fruit of the vine, or the extension of Christ's Life through you, (*John 15:7*).

In *Galatians 4:19*, we find that Paul prayed from a broken state in his own life for them, (the Galations), to be contrite before God. Virtually, he said that we must be willing to let God take over our lives. Please understand that he was talking only to Christians. These were born-again believers. They had already found Christ as their Savior. Paul further longed for them to be transformed to the Image of Christ by the Holy Spirit, that they be brought alive by the Power of His Glory. Then, that which reigned within them could, by their personal choice, rule and govern so that Christ's Ministry could be carried on through them. Men who will not seek God in fullness and travail in prayer will become religious by nature. They will become involved in what pleases their personal desire for a relationship with God. They will be more worried about the time than the times in which we live.

Until Christ is formed within us, there can never be a walk with God, (*Romans 8:1*), for the walk comes by the power of that formation. The Bible says it also in *I Thessalonians 2:9*, "*Remember, brethren, our labour and travail.*" This portion of the verse brings a tremendous witness to my heart.

Before we go to a Spiritual Warfare Prayer Seminar or Crusade, I always send the hosting church our preparation manual to use prior to our coming. These are planned activities to assure attendance and participation of the church at our meetings and to introduce our ministry. Now, I am not putting down the need for preparation; however, we have conducted crusades in which, prior to our arrival, the Spirit of God would be interworking in my heart. I would stand broken in the pulpit, anointed with the Power of God beyond anything that I had contrived or considered through our manuals.

As I look back on these marvelous experiences, I can remember one or two outstanding things about the meetings. The reasons for God's visitation was either the result of some great travail in my life, or I would discover in the course of the event that someone, (or more than one), had been brought under the burden of the gathering and God was extending His Power and Glory through him.

FIRST RATTLE OUT OF THE BOX

I'm reminded of a wonderful move of Grace that we experienced a number of years ago. I had been invited to come to an area north of Abilene, Texas to a "crossroads" church. The pastor was a very precious brother of God who had literally yielded his life to the Lord. We had been with him before in meetings and knew his love for God. Upon arrival on Saturday, I knew something was going on in my spirit. I asked the Pastor if there was anyone interceding for the revival. He said, "Brother Bonner, we have a woman here who is deeply broken and praying." I realized then what was going on in me. The first service was on Sunday morning. Their usual crowd attended. When I arose from my chair to speak, the Holy Spirit immediately began directing me to preach on a subject that I knew was taboo in trying to build a crowd. The message was on "Unforgiveness." It is definitely not your Sunday morning, crowd-pleasing, attention-getting, get-them-back tonight sermon, to say the least. I fought with the Holy Spirit in my spirit stating, "I'll run these people off." Again, I have a tendency to preach in anger when I am not anointed. And I thought, "Lord, we must have revival in this church. Do not make me do this." I could not convince God to go in another direction.

So, in hopeless obedience, while inside kicking and screaming, I turned in my Bible to begin the message in this particular area. *I John 2:8-11* says:

> *"Again a new commandment I write unto you which thing is true in Him and in you because the darkness has passed and the true light now shineth. He that sayeth that he is in the light and hateth his brother is in darkness even until now. He that loveth his brother abideth in the light and there is none occasion of stumbling in him. But he that hateth his brother is in darkness and walketh in darkness and knoweth not whether he goeth because darkness has blinded his eyes."*

To quote an old adage, the "first rattle out of the box" was the statement from my mouth to those Sunday morning Christians: "If you have anything in your heart against another Christian, not one prayer you pray is answered." Now, this is true in that if you have any resentments at all, God tells you that you cannot hear from Him. Unforgiveness is sin and the object of prayer is to be able to hear from God and correspond. You must know His Will in order to agree with Him that His Mind be performed through your life according to His Purpose.

Then I found myself moving to **Matthew Chapter 6**, to the two verses following the Lord's Prayer. I read these, then gave the truth of their meanings from the original Greek text: "If anyone has ever accidentally or willfully harmed you, and you have not given up resentment, God will not hear you as you pray." I then made the statement that, "You are never to take spiritual instruction from a person who is critical of another individual. Nor are you to ask that same person to pray, for he speaks by hearsay and not by revelation. He does not hear from God."

As we dove deeper into this, I was wondering, "Lord, what is going on?" As I looked across the faces of these people, there seemed to be deep shock. I wanted to preach a simple salvation message about Jesus. I was wondering how I could relieve the pressure and get out of this and still preserve this crowd for the rest of the meeting.

Then the Holy Spirit took it one step further. I asked a question, "How many of you here love God with all of your heart?" Most of them raised their hands. The next thing I knew I was quoting **I John 4:20**, which says:

> **"If a man says I love God and hateth his brother, he is a liar for he that loveth not his brother whom he has seen, how can he love God who he hath not seen?"**

Now, when you say the word "liar" to most Sunday morning Christians, it is an indictment. So, I knew I'd lost this crowd. It would be a miracle if they came back. "Oh, God, help!"

Then a worse thing happened. I suddenly found I was through. I looked at my watch. It was fifteen minutes to twelve. I had been preaching for less than fifteen minutes. I began to say to God in my spirit, "I cannot stop here. They expect a full message from this evangelist." I looked at the Pastor. His face showed no emotion. I was in trouble. If I stopped, I would anger people. If I went on, I would anger the Holy Spirit. I asked God what was going on. I knew in my spirit that I could not, under any circumstance, rescue what had already been done. I had never preached a fifteen minute message in my life. Quite the contrary. It is always forty-five minutes to an hour. However, I knew better than to fight what was going on in my spirit.

And so, I said, "I want you to stand and bow your heads." People were startled. Then I found myself making this statement: "I want you to stand" and, as they stood up, I wondered, "Lord, what's next?" He said, "Just wait." They began to play an invitation hymn as they do in this denominational structure; however, no one sang. I did not know what to say. I had not given an evangelistic summary for people to be born again. In my flesh I wanted to make something happen to at least attempt to save the meeting.

I was, needless to say, totally frustrated. This whole thing was out of my control. Then, in the very back of the church, I saw movement. There was a woman crying, who bolted out of her pew and went across the aisle to another and threw her arms around her. The lady who was suddenly embraced by the broken one was startled, then her face showed anger, and then it melted with the emotion of breaking, and she started to cry. Both of them were sobbing on each other's shoulder.

Instantly, from all over the auditorium, people began to move out of their seats and come forward. I thought to myself, "What's going on here?" More continued to come, verse after verse. It was glorious! God anointed the service with His Presence. People were born again.

God's Power came again that night. When I first walked in, I was startled by the number of those who had come. By numbers, it was the same crowd that had attended morning worship. This never happens. All of the Sunday morning Christians had come back. The Pastor, at lunch, had affirmed the desperate need for these two ladies to respond to each other. They had hated one another over the years, and it had caused a deep division in that body of believers.

As I stood to preach that evening, I was devoid of a message. I had waited all afternoon for some great revelation from God to try to rebuild the crowd through the Presence of His Spirit. But, nothing would come. It was not until I stood to preach that God gave me a message and people were again saved. It was wonderful.

When I arrived on Monday evening for the service, I was astounded again. The building was filled. The Power of God was in the music and His Presence filled the atmosphere. There were many young people in attendance on a school night, which was an amazing thing in this day and time because they, for the most part, have abandoned our churches. I began to speak in an anointed way. It was not me and I knew it. Again, souls were saved and lives were changed.

On Tuesday evening, the building was once again filled. It was startling. All through that day, I had sought God for a message and could hear nothing from Him as I prayed. Later, in analyzing the meeting, I realized that He was showing me that it is His Holy Spirit that works and not man, and, only in answer to prayer. It is well said, "That which comes nearest omnipotence is, impotence." Here I am again, it's Tuesday night and I am standing before that crowd with nothing to say. I began by welcoming the congregation. Meanwhile, I am thumbing through my Bible, begging God for a Scripture that would arrest my heart so I could launch out into God's message. I was so fearful that I would do something to ruin the meeting. I knew from past experience in my life that because I did desire His Presence, something would happen in whatever He gave me. I stood in trepidation, which is actually the beginning of God's Will. I was there for at least two minutes, thumbing, hoping, begging, looking through the pages. People were looking at me, waiting. Finally, I had to say to the people, "Folks, I am sorry. I do not have a word from God and I am not going to touch this meeting with anything from me."

I looked across the faces of that jammed building and finally heard myself say, "If some of you would like to come forward and pray, please come now." It was like I had yelled fire and the exit to the building was behind the pulpit. People came out of their pews, got on their knees, and had completely covered the front of that church, praying. They also took up the center aisle halfway to the back. I thought again to myself, "God, what are you up to now!" I waited, pleading with God to do something or at least tell me what to do.

Then after about five minutes, I said, "If there is anyone here who has a word, would you share it now?" The key leader in that church was a deacon. He was a man involved in everything. He had been on the second row for the entire meeting. Now, he was directly in front of me, just to my right on his knees, at the altar praying with his wife. Suddenly, he jumped up, and with tears streaming down his cheeks, he confessed before that entire body, adultery in his life. He apologized and sought forgiveness of the church for living two lives. He turned to his wife and while weeping said to her, "I beg your forgiveness! I love you! Can you ever forgive me?" Now, this woman stood up and threw her arms around her husband and they both fell to their knees sobbing. Now, please understand. To admit something this grave in nature, it must be spontaneous from the Lord. If it isn't, it will damage the church, as well as all involved, thereby giving place to Satan.

In the meantime I thought to myself, "God, what are you up to?" Soon another person stood up in that crowd and began to openly confess sin. God broke over him as he yielded to the Lord. Then, on the second row, a boy about ten years old was standing. He was at the end of the pew at the aisle. He was holding onto the side of the seat and was rocking back and forth like he was about to fall. His problem was that he was crying so hard he could barely stand. When he finally got his breath, he cried out, "I have got to be saved!" His soul was in deepest agony for Christ.

Immediately, the man directly in front of me, just to my right who had just confessed to adultery, heard the voice of his own son, stood and began to crawl over that mass of people until he got to his child. He threw his arms around him and on their knees in that pew that father led his boy to Jesus Christ. I thought again, "What else could happen?" This thing was totally out of my control, praise the Lord!

Then, across that crowd, one by one, people began to stand and openly confess their sins. The Power of God was so strong in that place that all I could do was just wait in awe and watch His Presence and Glory in a way that I had read about for years, but had only experienced a few times in all of my ministry. Then, to top it all off, every fourth or fifth person would cry out, "I've got to be saved." It was wondrous! Not only were they jammed down all the aisles praying, but there was still at least one-half of that congregation seated in the pews. By this time, when I looked at my watch it was close to ten o'clock. No one had left. The Presence of God was incomprehensible.

Then there was a man with his wife that I had watched during this encounter with the Holy Spirit. He was about halfway back and also seated on the aisle. He had very intently looked and listened for that entire time. He finally said to me, "Brother Bonner, you don't know me but I was formerly the pastor of this church, and they ran me off." I saw heads begin to bob up and down in agreement, especially of those who were on their knees. Then he said, "I've held deep bitterness against one man who instigated their firing me." He then looked across the auditorium to the outside aisle. There was a small group of people who had sat in that entire service with their heads bowed, occasionally looking up. On the outside seat was an elderly man, with his wife next to him, along with another couple. This former pastor was looking in his direction and finally crossed over, and through those praying, came around next to him. He was then broken and weeping. He got on his knees and put his arm around this deacon and laid his head on his shoulder and wept and asked him to forgive his bitterness. The deacon, with his head bowed, had yet to acknowledge he was even there.

Almost instantly, another person stood and said, "I must be saved," and soon someone was at his side leading him to Christ. And then another glorious thing happened. Almost to the back was a young man of about eighteen whom I had observed, watching all that was happening, very intently. He stood up and said, "I've hated God. I've hated this church. But I've seen tonight that God is real." He then said, "I must be saved."

You say, "What was so wonderful about that, other than the wonder of his salvation?" It had been happening all evening. The miracle of it was that the former pastor who was weeping on the shoulder of the deacon heard the sound of the voice of his young, rebellious son who had totally turned his back upon God, having experienced what the church had done to his dad. He jumped up and ran around the back of that building, and they met in the aisle and embraced and sobbed together and fell on their knees and began to pray. He was gloriously saved as he was led to Christ by his father.

Beloved friend, this went on and on until past midnight and not one person had left the service. That's what a real revival looks like. I was astounded and reminded again that when two people are upset with each other the spirit of division has moved into the church body by Satan. When they got right with each other, God's Spirit fell. Forgiveness is the door to God's visitation.

Now, that's not the end of the story. More miracles occurred on Wednesday night. I arrived at the church early. When I drove into the parking lot, it was filled. The first thought that came across my mind was, "They had a meal here tonight and no one told me." And you that know me know that I do not miss a meal, especially in a country setting! I walked into the church to find the Pastor and ask why I wasn't invited to eat, and to my utter amazement, for a service that was to start at 7:30 p.m., at 7:00 the building was about half full.

I looked at those folks, and I didn't recognize anyone from the meeting. As I stated earlier, I have a tendency to preach in anger and many times suffer a very serious carnal malady that I call "athlete's mouth," (my foot therein). That is, I speak without being spoken through. For when I first saw this crowd, the thought occurred to me, these are members of this church who have not attended this meeting since Sunday morning and have finally come back on Wednesday night. So I decided to play God. In my fleshly ire, I came to the first well-dressed couple seated next to the aisle, extended my hand, and said with authority, "Hello, my name is Mickey Bonner. Are you a member of this church?" I was ready to say to them, "Where have you been? Why haven't you been in the move of God's Glory here? You have missed God. Shame on you for not supporting your meeting. "

However, before I was able to do this, I was not ready for the answer he gave me. The man grabbed my hand and shook it and he said, "Oh, you're the preacher." I said, "Yes, sir." I was still feeling indignity. He said "No, we're not members here. In fact, we live over fifty miles away, but we got a call today from some folks who are members in this church, and they said if we would like to see what real revival looks like that we needed to come to their church tonight.

My beloved friend, most of those people in that room had been contacted by members of that church to come and see what it was like when God moved upon people. For the most part, they were visitors. I was overwhelmed. Then God spoke to my heart and said, **"When My Power comes, so will the people,"** (*Acts 2:46*). God broke over that church, and yet lest we take credit for anything that happened there, I must share with you that I was never allowed by God to preach any message that I wanted to preach. I stood in the pulpit several times devoid of anything other than the knowledge that God's Spirit and Presence was there. And I was totally terrified that I would destroy it with my taking over. So all that happened in those days must be taken in the right perspective. Remember when I first arrived, I asked the pastor about preparation for the meeting and if anyone was praying. The pastor said, "One woman is really broken over this meeting." There was the secret. It was the answer and is still the only answer. Broken praying. It is tragic today that in our churches we have programs to do what only real revival would do, and that is to bring people in. We are doing it backwards. God will fill our churches if we are broken before Him.

Christian, when we begin to travail or, in other words, sense what God feels in a matter, it is then, by that Power of His Glory through our earthen vessels that the Spirit of God begins to move. Until there is the labor of brokenness, this nation and this world system will never know a visitation from God. The days will become darker as we come closer to our Christ's return. Religion will befit the primary position that government desires, and there will be a one-world group that will become politically correct and accepted. Then, true Christianity will have no part in its function, though they will speak of the name of Jesus and His teachings, as well as the other deities people worship. They will see Jesus Christ as a prophet, but not Priest and King.

This is all a part of Satan's plan to destroy the Kingdom of God and Christ from the lives of all. My beloved, we can slow this inevitable process. It is promised. There can be a move of God's Powerful Glory and Spirit hindering this move of Satan until Jesus comes. We can see millions saved before the ultimate falling of all systems, whether they be political or religious, to Satan's power and his anti-Christ. If we will become humble before God and seek His face, *Isaiah 53:11* says, *"He shall see of the travail of his soul and shall be satisfied."* We must be broken before the Lord and we must have revival before Christ's return. We MUST. If we do not, we will leave close to five billion souls to burn in hell.

Brokenness is the answer. God states in *I Thessalonians 2:9*, *"Remember, brethren, our labor and travail.*" We also have the verse in *Isaiah 59:16* that says:

> "*And he saw that there was no man and wondered that there was no intercessor, therefore, his arm brought salvation unto him; and his righteousness, it sustained him.*"

Therein lies the tragedy of today. People are working in their concept of religious Christianity, but it is only by God's Power through us that true ministry comes. And He cannot intercede until we are broken. He must work through us, not us working for Him. But until we are as *Psalm 119:53* declares, "*Horror had taken hold upon me because of the wicked that forsake thy law,*" it will not come. We are blind leading the blind.

People today are so bound within the odyssey of the age in which we live. They are, as *Revelation 3:17* states, "*Increased with goods and have need of nothing.*" Therefore, their souls bear no real burden except for an occasional event in their own lives that comes from despair, discouragement, rebellion of children, illness, or financial bondage. Oh, my beloved, you must understand that these experiences either bring us to brokenness or bitterness. As one person has written, "We're either humbled or hardened."

Another illustration of this is in the life of Moses. The Bible states in *Numbers 12:3, "Now the man Moses was very meek, above all the men which were on the face of the earth."*

Alexander Whyte writes in Bible Characters:

"By all accounts, Moses did not begin by being a meek man. The truth is no truly meek man ever does so begin. It is not true meekness if it is found in any man at the beginning of his life. It may be sloth, it may be softness, it may be easiness, it may be indifference, it may be policy and calculation, it may be insensibility of heart, it may be sluggishness of blood, but true meekness it is not. True meekness it is not until it has been planted and watered, and pruned and purified, and beaten upon by every wind of God, and cut to pieces by every knife of God, and all the time engrafted and seated deep in the meekness and in the gentleness and in the humility of the Spirit of God and the Son of God.

It would be far nearer the truth to say that Moses, to begin with, was the hastiest and the hottest and the least meek and the least long-suffering of men. It was but a word and a blow with young Moses."

Beloved, God completely broke him. He drove him from his land and his people. For forty years, God prepared him for ministry. It took that period of humiliating reflection to yield to God. And yield he did. He was transformed into a man of faith, broken before God. He was humbled and not hardened.

I would to God that His Power so move upon our hearts as we hunger to be totally His, in order that He may operate through our brokenness. For it is when we are broken before men that God's Spirit begins to move. I'm reminded of what God says about the corn of wheat that is planted in the earth. You must know that before it is able to be sown, the soil must be broken. No farmer would broadcast seed upon hard ground. He would first wait for the season. Then, he would take the soil and pulverize it. From there, he would make a row and finally plant the seed and cover it up. Then he would wait for rain unless he could artificially bring moisture through irrigation. This, however, is only the beginning of the next step. The seed then has to go through a process within itself to reproduce. First of all, it has to die. Death always occurs before new life. In the case of revival, it is the death of the soul by crucifixion in the life of an individual wanting to go on with God. For out of that dead body on the cross bursted forth, by the Spirit of God, Life eternal and everlasting. God states we must be crucified with Christ and spiritually resurrected by His Life, (**Romans 12:1; Galatians 2:20**). By the same token, the elements in that dark earth begin to do a work upon that planted seed as it provides moisture and nutrition. Then, something is born inside the seed as it begins to break, like a baby chick from its embryonic stage coming to full term, suddenly beginning to peck from the interior side of the shell. So does this happen to the seed itself; while in the midst of its darkest time, it bursts forth to come to new life. The outer shell then begins to break and soon the husk or old man is pushed aside.

In God's design, that small sprout continues to force itself in the right direction. Finally, it breaks through the soil and sees the first ray of light. A new process begins at that point. Light itself is a nutrient to its life as it daily faces the sun. The delicate plant continues to grow upward while the root system plunges deeper to take its needed sustenance, increasing more of the life that it has been given at that point.

Then it comes to great victory as the purpose for its being is realized, producing multiple fruit of its own kind through the power that has been given it from the process of death, birth, and life. This is spoken of in **John 12:23-25** where it says:

"And Jesus answered them saying, 'The hour is come that the Son of Man should be glorified.

Verily, verily, I say unto you, except a corn of wheat fall into the ground and die, it abideth alone; but if it die, it bringeth forth much fruit. He that loveth his life shall lose it. And he that hateth his life in this world shall keep it unto life eternal'."

Furthermore, the process of death to self brings the Life of Christ to and through us. We must, however, be desirous to be crucified with Christ. We must go to the field of prayer and be ready to be planted in brokenness, that this outer husk may be torn away and the inner life of the Holy Spirit may come out. We will bear the fruit of righteousness.

George Stringer Rowe wrote a poem that enhances our reading:

> Blessed Savior, Christ most holy,
> In a manger Thou didst rest;
> Canst thou stoop again, yet lower
> And abide within my breast?
>
> Enter, then, O Christ most holy,
> Make a Christmas in my heart.
> Make a Heaven of my manger,
> It is Heaven where Thou art.

THE SERVANT'S REWARD

One of the great tragedies in Christendom today is the teaching of the activity of the flesh in order to bring Christ's ministry alive. Probably the best statement against it is found in *John 15*. God begins with, *"The father is the husband. Jesus is the vine, we are the branches."* He states that when we choose to take hold of the vine and abandon our lives to it, (Jesus), and become engrafted in it, (Jesus), God becomes the husbandman. As the husbandman-vine dresser, He prunes the non-fruit producing limbs to keep them from taking life from the vine.

Any person that has ever raised roses or tomatoes knows what it means to prune the vines. For you do not raise them for the beauty of the plant, you plant them for the fruit or the flower. Understand that the vine takes the branch anywhere it wants to place it. Our lives are His in obedience. Then, in our holding daily onto that vine through prayer, Jesus begins to produce His life through us. Through the branch of the Christian comes the Life and Ministry of Christ, for this is the Fruit itself. The fruit of a Christian is not the producing of another Christian. It is the person of Jesus Christ producing His Life through a Christian.

The proof of His control of your life is when people partake of that fruit of your witness or prayer. They do not look at you later and say, "Oh wonderful branch." They declare, "Oh, glorious vine. Oh, Precious Jesus Christ." When you get home to heaven, you will receive from Jesus the servant's reward. You say, "Brother Bonner, what do I get out of that kind of an environment here on earth?" You get the life of the vine in and through you, which is love, joy, peace, and all of the attributes of *Galatians 5:22-24*. It is *"Christ in you, the hope of Glory."* He is *"name above every name."* For it is only through that relationship and effort that fruit is given.

Oswald Chambers wrote:

"Blessed are the tamed, the balanced, the disciplined, the God-controlled, the teachable, the Pilgrims of the middle road of God, the giants who by

- 240 -

the Spirit resist every impulse and set in motion and harness every good inclination to the Glory of God. For they shall rule as kings and reign as lords in the regeneration of all things."

Incidentally, **John 15** also states that, "God will collect the branches of those who have separated themselves from the vine who bear their own fruit (religion) and burn them." Please understand that at the Judgment Seat of Christ your works will be burned, and God will sift through what remains. The ash represents the religious works of your life: the wood, hay, and stubble. It will all be burned away. The works of religious flesh are Christians doing Christian activities based on the concept of man. If in the burning there is gold, silver, and precious stones, it will be the result of the ministry of God's Spirit in and through your life. Please remember that gold and silver are produced by pressure, heat, and mineral combined. Precious stones, (such as the diamond), are the strongest of all formations. This comes from the hottest fire and the strongest force, similar to the pressure involved in volcanic activity. Such activity produces the most beautiful of all gems. When it is broken, and facets are ground, the light is shone into them. There is an explosion of brilliance and color. The greater the pressure and intensity of heat, the purer the diamond.

In Chapter One, I referred to the following poem. After having read this entire book, I believe it is most fitting for you to grasp it once again. It was submitted to me by my secretary, Diana Taylor. The author is unknown:

"One by one He took them from me,
All the things I valued most,
'Til I was empty-handed,
Every glittering toy was lost.

And I walked earth's highways, grieving,
In my rags and poverty,
Until I heard His voice inviting,
'Lift those empty hands to Me!'

Then I turned my hands toward heaven,
And He filled them with a store
Of His own transcendent riches,
'Til they could contain no more.

And at last I comprehended,
With my stupid mind, and dull,
That God cannot pour His riches
Into hands already full."

Christ shines His Light in the life of the broken believer and through him, into the areas of the darkness of this world. Through the facets of breaking comes out of us the true light. It draws attention to the flame and not the candle. We must be broken before God or we will never be used of Him.

Another example of this is given to us by Spurgeon. He writes:

"Humiliation of soul always brings a positive blessing with it. If we empty our hearts of self, God will fill them with His love. He who desires a close communion with Christ should remember the Word of the Lord, 'To this man will I look, even to him that is poor and of a contrite spirit, and trembleth at my Word.' Stoop if you would climb to Heaven. Do we not say of Jesus, 'He descended that He might ascend? So must you. You must grow downwards that you may grow upwards; for the sweetest fellowship with Heaven is to be had by humble souls, and by them alone. God will deny no blessing to a thoroughly humbled spirit."

Another example of that kind of brokenness is the Biblical account of Mary of Bethany, found in *Matthew 26:6-13*. It begins:

> *"When Jesus was in Bethany in the House of Simon the Leper, there was a woman that came with an alabaster box full of precious ointment and poured it on his head as he sat at meat or eating."*

Now, as you study this, you will find that His disciples were filled with indignation because of the deed. Their response was, *"Could this have been sold and given to the poor?"*

People so soon forget that God owns the cattle of a thousand hills and when we are in the midst of His Plan, operating according to His Purpose and His Will, He will always finance what He begins. I have discovered, after many years of being disciplined, that if God is involved in a matter, the finances will come. A man's gift will make way for itself, (*Proverbs 18:16*). These disciples were angry at what they felt was a waste. Then He stated to His Disciples, *"Quit complaining about this woman. She hath wrought a good work upon me."*

Now, there was a custom at that time that a body was anointed for burial. This dear woman had begun preparing Christ for His death upon the cross. He said in her behalf, *"Where the Gospel is preached from now on, this shall be a memorial to her life forever."* The truth of this matter is that this woman, who came out of the deepest of sin because of an encounter with the Son of God, gave all she had. This is the result of a broken individual. He transfers and abandons ownership of everything he has and gives it back to God. Such is the title of this chapter, *"The Consent of Tribulation."* It is an endeavor of love and not obedience to the law. It is an overwhelming desire to go on with God.

Any that move to the process of true living, learn to give. In fact, you live at the level in which you give. When you have transferred ownership of all you have back to God, beginning with your life, it is at His direction that the verse *"give and it shall be given unto you,"* comes to life. This woman had learned victory. She had experienced pure, abandoned grace. And, most of all, she had undergone forgiveness and the involvement of the transformed life. So, it meant nothing to take that which she had earned by her trade to use to anoint Jesus for His death. It was a demonstration of her love and worship, poured out.

Christianity means being joyfully poured out. Religion is the constant pouring in. In fact, based on today's wage, the cost of that anointment was about $15,000 in American currency at this writing. Her ointment was very costly to the flesh and yet this woman was wondrously broken before the Lord. She gave it all. You must understand that when you are broken before God, you will hold on to nothing. You will abandon all that you have in order to walk with the Spirit of God. You will then move out of this life and begin to live in the position of the transformed kingdom's life here on Earth. The Bible says in *Mark 14:7-8*:

> *"For you have the poor with you always and whensoever you will you may do them good; but Me you have not always. She hath done what she could, she has come aforehand to anoint my body to the burying."*

Can you imagine what it was like when she got home to heaven? She was very likely received like the widow who gave two mites to the offering, (*Mark 12:42*).

As we study further about the brokenness of this woman before Christ, we find in *Luke 7:38*:

"She stood at His feet behind Him weeping, and began to wash his feet with tears, and did wipe them with the hairs of her head and kissed his feet and anointed them with the ointment."

Now, the Scripture goes on to say that as the Pharisee observed this, he said to himself, *"If this man Jesus was truly a prophet, He would have known who it was that touched Him for she is a sinner."* Having known the thoughts of Simon, Jesus then responded, *"I have somewhat to say unto thee."* And he said, *"Master say on."* Then he talks about a *"creditor which had two debtors, the one owed five hundred pence and the other fifty."* And when they had nothing to pay, He forgave their debt. Then He asked the question: *"Tell me, therefore, which of them will love him most?"* Simon answered and said, *"I suppose that he to whom He forgave most."* And He said unto him, *"Thou hast rightly judged."*

My beloved friend, I have observed many times over the years that believers who came out of the darkest areas of sinful life, had the greatest walk with God because they were so grateful for the transforming power of Jesus Christ in their lives. They are literally broken before the Lord. In the process of growth in Christ, they become so profoundly anointed and moved upon by the Spirit of God, that His Glory shines through the joyous brokenness of their hearts.

I am reminded of a woman who is the epitome of this Biblical story. Both my wife Margaret and I tried to minister to her some years ago when she was fourteen years of age. She came to us in a revival meeting in the port area in Houston. Her name was Iris Urray. She was at that time over six feet tall. She was a very beautiful girl, and my ministry to her was not only to share Christ, but to also say to her, "Please do not let your size be a hindrance to your life. Accept how God has made you to His Glory." What I was not aware of was that, even at that time, she was already into prostitution. I lost contact with her after that meeting only to be reacquainted many years later, after she had spent a period of time institutionalized in the Women's Penitentiary in Huntsville, Texas. She had become a criminal. Because of her size, she could overpower any guard in the place. They put her in solitary confinement and kept her there for a long season because she was, by the state's standard, incorrigible. Nothing could be done with her.

After a number of years, she was released, having served her full time without parole. She went back to the streets of Houston and again began to operate in prostitution, but this time with her own stable of girls. She moved deeper into sin and the darkness of the world's system. It was not in God's Will, however, for her to remain in that condition. So many had prayed for her. Finally, in God's timing, she had an encounter with a young evangelist who would not cease in praying for her until she was born again. She tried every way in the world to destroy his witness, but it would not work. She could not pull him down. Then, one day, she was gloriously redeemed by the Blood of the Lamb. Since then, Iris has become a living testimony of the Grace of God. She has traveled a number of times with us to Israel, and through her unique testimony, she constantly won people to Christ. She even testified to the Israeli guards who were going through her bags. Her story is unique. But it is a story of an individual who submitted all that she was to Christ, and in total abandonment Jesus became the sufficiency of her life. She was truly like the "woman at the well."

One day, through God-ordained circumstances, she met a man. Having been through all she had been through in her lifetime as a prostitute and on the streets, she immediately became burdened for his soul. She began to pray for him. This man was a biker living out of an old school bus. His background was like hers, very sordid and very sinful. Eventually, he, through the testimony of Iris, while literally kicking and screaming against all she was trying to do in his life, came into the Kingdom of God and was born from above. He was gloriously saved. His name is Dwayne Blue. Later on, they married and are still traveling worldwide, now giving their wonderful testimonies together.

They later had a baby, (which is a miracle in the sense that her body had been so abused over the years the doctors had told her she could never have children). But, God in His miraculous way, gave them a beautiful boy, and they named him "Denim." That's right, his name is Denim Blue. He already has a "cross to bear" in his lifetime! How many times have I been asked by people who would not believe that my first name was really Mickey: "Was it not Michael?" I even had a man say to me, "No one in their right mind would ever name their son Mickey." And then, later on, a dear friend of ours to whom we had ministered, (and she experienced victory), later married a man that she had met on one of our trips to Europe. Later, they had a son. Because our lives had been a part of her change for Christ, she decided she was going to name him after me. On the phone she asked the question, "What is your real name?" When I said, "My real name is Mickey," she said, "Are you sure it is not Michael?" I said, "I am sure." Then, after a long silence, she said in passing, "I would never name my son that," and hung up. So much for pride. To quote a phrase, "What's in a name?" Hang on, Denim.

Now, let me say to you as we have gone through this Scriptural account in the Book of Luke: This woman was so broken that the tears flooded down her cheeks and off her body onto the dusty feet of the Son of God. They were in such abundance that she was able to take the long hair from her head -- the badge of her trade as a prostitute, and wipe His feet. How precious the experience! For you see, I've been in church services where people have been from Christian homes and their lives were designed and developed around Christianity from their childhood. They knew the work of the cross. Upon hearing the Word, they trusted Christ when they were nine, ten, eleven, or twelve years of age. They literally, by osmosis, moved into God's Kingdom because they were raised and trained in believing in the things of God and His Christ. And then I've met those who have profoundly come out of the dregs of life, who upon exploding through the door of Salvation by Grace through Faith into the Kingdom of God, could not lay the cross down. They prayed night and day, and the grace and graciousness of God was so profound that He was the center of every conversation that they had. Those kinds of folks scare the average Christian. Most Christians don't like to be around people who speak of Jesus in the present tense and that walk constantly in His Will. In the light of this, it is interesting to note *Luke 7:44-48* that states:

> *"And He turned unto the woman and said unto Simon, 'Seest thou this woman? I entered into thine house, and thou gavest me no water for my feet; but she hath washed my feet with tears, and wiped them with the hairs of her head. Thou gavest me no kiss; but this woman, since the time I came in, hast not ceased to kiss*

my feet. My head with oil thou didst not anoint; but this woman hath anointed my feet with ointment. Wherefore I say unto thee, her sins which are many are forgiven; for she loved much; but to whom little is forgiven the same loveth little.' And He said unto her, 'Thine sins are forgiven'."

Now, can you imagine the profoundness of that statement in the presence of those men? I want you now to see in your spirit mind where she was. Kneeling and in broken worship in the presence of Jesus, her sins were forgiven. Her life was cleansed, and if she thought she could totally worship Him then, she was far mistaken. For you must understand that right after death or rapture, when we see Him as He is and we know Him for what He has done in our glorified minds, we will cry *"worthy is the Lamb!"*

Oh, my beloved, I beg you by the Blood of Jesus Christ and by the Power of His Name that you will pray to be broken; that you will pray to see yourself as you really are and ask God to break you until there is nothing remaining but Jesus. There must be the "consent of tribulation" in your life. For, again, the trip is not calamity or catastrophe, but it is joyful union and reunion with Him who made you and wants to live His life through you.

It is tragic that very few Christians know the joy of being broken into the Life of Christ. Not many have ever come to that place. Those that did, however, changed the world around them. Also, one thing that you understand is that when brokenness is present in the hearts of a congregation, you can walk into the building where they are assembled and God's presence is overwhelming. The Spirit of God is atmospheric.

I belong to a church in Houston and when you drive on the campus you can experience the Presence of God's Glory. When you go into its worship service, the Holy spirit is there, even before the music begins to present high praises to God. The message to the people has the anointing of God's Power. Now, the secret to our church is no secret at all. The fact is that there is a twenty-four hour, seven day a week, prayer room where prayer warriors pray. They sign up to donate one or more hours a week at specific times. My pastor is a man of God and one whom I deeply love and have submitted my ministry to for covering. When he stands to preach there is a power that comes only from God. I might add that he is a broken man who is deeply in love with the Lord. The attributes of his life, however, are not only in the ministry of that church where he's been for many years, but also in his family. All of his children serve the Lord full time. That kind of heritage is a sign of true brokenness.

Now, in regard to the woman with the perfume, the Bible teaches that when she broke that alabaster box and poured it over the head of Jesus, it poured down upon His beard, (as Aaron's beard of *Psalm 133:2* and *Exodus 30:30*), and the house filled with the aroma. The sweet smelling presence of this anointment mingled with the Glory of the Son of God.

Incidentally, the disciples disapproved of what she was doing and tried to get her away from Jesus. We find in *Mark 14:6*, *"And Jesus said to these men, let her alone, why trouble ye her, she hath wrought a good work on me."* If you have consented to tribulation by asking God to break you, it is for the purpose in your heart to wrought a good work upon Christ. As Jesus was wounded and spilled out, so are we to be broken before God, that the continual flow of His Spirit to and through us will move into the lives of other people. I cannot emphasize any stronger this verse that I trust that God will one day make to those reading this volume. When you get home some day, I hope you will hear, *"Well done, thou good and faithful servant."*

Pray that God will break you. Become a living sacrifice, HOLY, acceptable. It is your reasonable service, (*Romans 12:1*).

IN CONCLUSION

The word brokenness has such a final sound to it, and yet it is only the beginning. It is one of the great paradoxes of the Bible. There are paradoxes in the Word, such as "you live by dying," "you receive by giving," "you become strong when you become weak," "you win by losing," and "you succeed by failing." These truths to the carnal mind carry no focus to reality; therefore, in being denied, they are never experienced. Such is the position of brokenness. Its very connotation is rejected because of Satan's accusation of the price to be paid. And yet the greatest joy one will ever know is the joy of Jesus Christ controlling from within. This is experienced only in the abandoned heart toward God. In this event we face what we really are from the perspective of what God sees, and with abhorrence we deny its rule over us; therefore, becoming "a living sacrifice." God then fills us with the Holy Spirit to that level of brokenness. We are overwhelmed with His Glory and Love through us.

This is the deepest form of Christianity, and it is the true beginning of all ministry in the person's life. All events before this are activities of religion. All through this place of the Cross, is the True Work of God through the person. It is the crossover of the Jordan into the land of the milk and honey spoken of in the Old Testament. It is a place of joy in the midst of the storm.

It is the true location of peace that passeth all understanding. And, though we live in the midst of a dying world that will see in its lifetime the coming of Christ, we can, in Him, have "**joy unspeakable and full of Glory.**" It is truly the Place of Grace.

Make this your choice beginning right now. First, you must confess any known sin to God. Second, you must forgive all who have harmed or hurt you in any way, (*Matthew 5:44*). Third, you must seek to be broken and filled with the Holy Spirit. Fourth, you must labor daily to remain in that position with Him by fighting your own flesh, making yourself study the Bible and pray, and also keeping your mouth and ears shut from all that would destroy your walk with God.

And then, as I have stated many times, you must present your body as a living sacrifice that you might receive the Mind, Life, and Will of the Father, (*Romans 12:1-2*). No one can do it for you. It must be by force that you come into the place of rest with God.

Revival will never come until this happens. I beg you to let it happen to you. Begin your life's adventure by choosing today to be broken before the Lord. Pray for it. Fast for it. Whatever it takes to break through to God's Throne, do it to His Glory. It is "your reasonable service" as you become Holy as He is Holy in you. It is not you, but Him. It is "Christ in you, the Hope of Glory."

"Choose you this day whom ye will serve."

It is your choice, whether it be the flesh of religion or the Spirit of God. If it is for Christ's Control, then begin by praying this prayer:

"Father, in the Name of Jesus Christ, I choose you today. Whatever it takes to break me, do it. I must be Yours completely. I am ready for Your Life in and through me.

In Jesus Christ's Name,

Amen."

And now, begin to praise Him in faith believing, for here comes Life in its abundance. Now, begin to pray for revival for you are in the position of *II Chronicles 7:14*, humbled. Now, God will "hear" and "heal." God bless you and keep praying.

Mickey Bonner

RECOMMENDED BOOKS AND AUTHORS
ON THE SUBJECT OF BROKENNESS

Baldwin, Lindley. The Life Story of Samuel Morris, Bethany Fellowship.

Billheimer, Paul E. Destined For The Throne, Christian Literature Crusade, 1979.

Drummond, Lewis. The Awakening That Must Come, Broadman Press, 1979.

Drummond, Lewis. The Greatest Thing In The World.

Drummond, Lewis. The Revived Life, Broadman Press, 1982.

Edwards, Jonathan. The Life Of Reverend David Brainerd, Baker Book House, 1978.

Finney, Charles G. Prevailing Prayer, Kregel, 1965.

Grubb, Norman. Continuous Revival, Christian Literature Crusade.

Grubb, Norman. Rees Howells: Intercessor, Christian Literature Crusade.

Harvey, Edward and Lillian. Royal Insignia, Harvey and Tait.

Hession, Roy. My Calvary Road, Christian Literature Crusade.

Mueller, George. Answers To Prayer, Moody Press.

Murray, Andrew. Humility, Whitaker.

Murray, Andrew. The Believer's School Of Prayer, Bethany House.

Murray, Andrew. The Ministry Of Intercession, Fleming H. Revell.

Nee, Watchman. The Normal Christian Life, Christian Literature Crusade.

Orr, J. Edwin. The Flaming Tongue, Moody Press.

Ravenhill, Leonard. Why Revival Tarries, Bethany Fellowship.

Taylor, Jack. The Key to Triumphant Living, Broadman Press.

Tozer, A. W. The Knowledge Of The Holy, Harper and Row.

The Unknown Christian. The Kneeling Christian, Zondervan.